Instant Library Lessons

First Grade

Karen A. Farmer Wanamaker

UpstartBooks

Fort Atkinson, Wisconsin

To my husband Boyce, who knew I could do this long before I ever dreamed I even wanted to.

Published by UpstartBooks
W5527 State Road 106
P.O. Box 800
Fort Atkinson, Wisconsin 53538-0800
1-800-448-4887

© Karen A. Farmer Wanamaker, 2005
Cover design and illustrations by Debra Neu

The paper used in this publication meets the minimum requirements of
American National Standard for Information Sciences —
Permanence of Paper for Printed Library Materials. ANSI/NISO Z39.48-1992.

Contents

❁ Introduction ❁

When I was in college preparing to become a Library Media Specialist, I had no idea how important my experiences with and love for designing curriculum would become. Once I reached the real world I quickly realized that everyone in an elementary school had textbooks, workbooks, teachers' editions, or at the very least, a list of objectives—everyone, that is, except the Library Media Specialist.

Through the years I searched for a source of lesson plans that provided for the needs of Library Media Specialists and their students. In the meantime I created my own lessons. This was actually a plus as I truly enjoyed the creative process. Unfortunately, there was never enough time to fully develop the lesson ideas with all that had to be done in the library. Now I have the opportunity to do what I always thought someone ought to do. This book is designed to provide a year's worth of lessons—all that is needed are the suggested books and the children.

These lessons were specifically designed to support the following educational beliefs:

• Instruction should include exposure to fiction and nonfiction at all levels.

• Learning experiences are most successful when taught in a consistent frame that moves learning from whole class instruction through teamwork and working in pairs before expecting children to work alone.

• In order for students to have the best opportunity to learn, adults should foster higher levels of thinking by asking questions that encourage thought and by teaching students to ask their own thought-provoking questions.

• Using children's literature to direct learning is most appropriate when addressing library instruction.

• Interactive instruction based on what is known about learning styles provides the best environment for learning.

• Library instruction should fully support the school-wide curriculum.

How to Use This Book

The length and number of library sessions varies greatly from library to library, and often from school year to school year within the same location. Many other factors, such as the number of students per class and the amount of checkout time needed, contribute to the amount of instructional time available in a library.

For these reasons, this book was designed to provide 36 one-hour lessons. Each lesson can be used in one session or broken into smaller segments for multiple sessions. These lessons offer Library Media Specialists choices in determining the makeup of their particular library class instruction.

The Instant Library Lessons series includes Lesson Learning Ideas that encompass the following instructional strands:

- **Library Skills:** Including, but not limited to, research and learning skills.

- **Literature Appreciation:** Exposure to and experience with a variety of print genres.

- **Techniques of Learning:** Strategies such as questioning skills and interactive learning that support lifelong learning.

- **Comprehension:** Developing learning processes that support effective readers and learners.

- **Writing Experiences:** Fostering the link between reading and writing needed throughout a lifetime.

- **Oral Language:** Opportunities to develop and refine skills in interpersonal communication from speaking, listening and viewing.

Each individual lesson includes:

- **Featured Book(s).** The book or books the lesson is based upon with corresponding summary information.

- **Lesson Learning Ideas.** Specific lesson objectives based on the instructional strands developed for Instant Library Lessons. See pages 12–14.

- **Materials.** Items to be collected prior to instruction. Ordering information is available (see pages 187–189 for details) so the needed items can be obtained as easily as possible.

- **Before Class.** A list of tasks to complete before teaching the lesson.

- **Lesson Plan.** Presented in a format that can be followed step by step or altered to meet your specific needs.

Suggested Library Set-Up

In order to fully implement all of the lesson ideas included in this book a sample room layout has been created (see page 11). Recommendations include:

- Library furniture that includes enough tables and chairs to accommodate all of the students from one class within a given area. Each table should have a permanent container (basket) with crayons or markers, scissors and glue. Additional items, such as books or lesson materials, can be added when necessary. A permanent table sign label will assist in giving directions to students.

- A gathering area that provides for a more intimate sharing of books and learning experiences. The gathering area will need a stool or chair for the librarian. The students can sit on the floor. A big book stand, overhead projector on a movable cart, screen, easel with chart paper or chalkboard, TV with VCR and/or DVD complete the needed equipment.

- Other items which help organize the library setting might include: a movable book return cart located near the library entrance; a movable cart or table for a container of shelf markers and to display check-out name cards in divided containers; and a place for free reading materials (this could be a section within existing book shelves and/or a table space and should have enough room to accommodate a laundry-sized basket and several smaller baskets).

Tips of the Trade

- **Ready Rhyme.** Whenever students are seated on the floor, teach them this rhyme to help them learn how to get ready to listen. You can use the sign language words provided to go with the rhyme. Repeat the rhyme with motions until all of the students are ready.

  If you are seated on your bottom, *(Sit)*
  With your legs crossed,
  And your eyes this way, *(Look)*
  You're ready, *(Ready)*
  You're ready,
  You're ready,
  Yea.

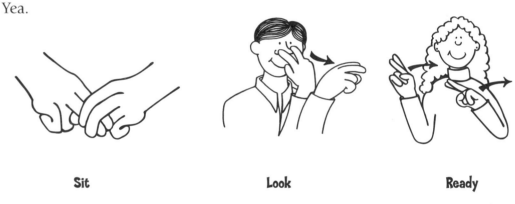

| Sit | Look | Ready |

- When you need to get your children's attention, teach them these words in sign language:

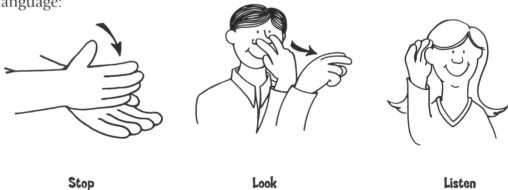

| Stop | Look | Listen |

Do not continue until every student is participating in the signing.

- When it is time for students to line up to leave the library call one table at a time. This can be done by labeling each table with a different color table sign. Then use sign language or a foreign language to instruct the students when it is their turn. For example, say and/or sign the following phrase:

  Red Table, line up slowly and quietly.

  Then, continue with yellow, green, blue, black, white, purple, orange or whatever colors you choose. Use one of the following Web sites to locate sign language information: *www.handspeak.com* or *www.mastertech-home.com/ASLDict.html.*

- In order to get a line of children all going in the same direction teach them to "ENT." (If your eyes, ears, nose and throat are facing the door you are ready to go!)

- **Wiggle Squeezers.** Often during instruction students will need to take a break. Use one or more of the following movement activities to provide a break.

Shake Your Sillies Out

<u>Verse 1</u>: *(Hold hands slightly above waist level with elbows bent at 90 degree angle. Rotate arms and hips from side to side in a twisting motion. On the last line of the verse, point index fingers while moving hands up and down at the wrist.)*
You've got to shake, shake, shake your sillies out.
Shake, shake, shake your sillies out.
Shake, shake, shake your sillies out.
And wiggle your waggles away.

<u>Verse 2</u>: Clap your crazies out. *(Clap hands on first three lines. On the last line of the verse, point index fingers while moving hands up and down at the wrist.)*

<u>Verse 3</u>: Stretch your stretchies out. *(Stretch arms in various directions on the first three lines. On the last line of the verse, point index fingers while moving hands up and down at the wrist.)*

<u>Verse 4</u>: Jump your jingles out. *(Jump up and down in place on the first three lines of the rhyme. On the last line of the verse, point index fingers while moving hands up and down at the wrist.)*

<u>Verse 5</u>: Yawn your yuckies out. *(Slow down the pace of the chant and speak softly during this verse. On the first three lines cover your mouth and yawn while inhaling during the word "yawn." On the last line of the verse, point index fingers while moving hands up and down at the wrist.)*

Hi, My Name is Joe

Hi, my name is Joe.
I've got a wife and three kids,
And I work in a button factory.
One day the boss came in,
He said, "Joe, are you busy?"
I said, "No."
He said, "Do it like this."

The first time just say the words. Then add a motion and repeat the words again while doing the motion. At the end of each verse, add an additional movement while continuing each of the previous movements.

Suggested movements: *Wave right hand; wave left hand; raise and lower one foot; march in place by raising and lowering each foot one at a time; and nod head. On the last verse change the words to: Joe, are you busy? I said, yes!*

Oliver Twist

Oliver, twist, twist, twist,
(Place your hands on your hips and twist side to side each time you say "twist.")
Can't do this, this, this, *(Stretch both arms high over head.)*
Touch your toes, toes, toes, *(Bend at the waist and touch your fingers to your toes.)*
Nobody nose, nose, nose.
(Place your right hand into your left palm and touch your nose with both hands.)

Say the rhyme three times, repeating it faster each time. Then do the rhyme one last time in extra slow motion to calm the children down.

Do Your Ears Hang Low?

Do your ears hang low? *(Backs of hands on ears, fingers down.)*
Do they wobble to and fro? *(Sway fingers.)*
Can you tie 'em in a knot? *(Tie large knot in air.)*
Can you tie 'em in a bow? *(Draw bow in air with both hands.)*
Can you throw 'em over your shoulder, *(Throw both hands over left shoulder.)*
Like a continental soldier? *(Salute.)*
Do your ears hang low? *(Backs of hands on ears, fingers down.)*

Always do the last verse in extra slow motion to calm the children down and prepare them to return to work.

- **Free Reading Area.** Throughout the lessons there are suggested materials for the "Free Reading Area." Note the map under suggested library set-up to see where to locate such materials. These are self-directed materials students can use when they have wait time. Wait time most often occurs during check out since all children can't select a book at the same time. Establish guidelines for using the materials within your library. Be sure to introduce and practice how to use the materials before they appear in the Free Reading Area.

Materials for a free reading area might include:

- Velcro boards, aprons and mitts with story pieces in plastic bags based on Literature Pictures

- metal boards with story pieces in plastic bags based on Literature Pictures

- minute books—brief, paperback books for early readers

- children's magazines

Add items as recommended in the lesson plans. Rotate items so students don't get bored with the offerings. House similar items in plastic baskets for easy access and clean up.

Literature Pictures (LPs)

Literature Pictures work well for presentations and Free Reading Area materials.

1. Make copies of the pictures.

2. Color the pictures. If coloring anything the size of your hand or smaller, it should be colored with the thick lead, colored art pencils. These can be found in art stores (Hobby Lobby or Michael's) or some school supply stores and catalogs. The brand that has been most successful is Prismacolor. If enlarging the pictures so they are larger than your hand, artist pastel chalks work well. After coloring, lightly spray the pictures with cheap hairspray. Most of the pastels found in school and art supply stores are fine for this activity.

3. Back each piece with poster board. Use spray glue, which is often called spray adhesive. This makes for a smooth finish and can be bought at paint and discount stores. Cut out the pieces.

4. Write any cues needed for telling the story on the back of the individual pieces. Then laminate and cut out the pieces.

5. Decide between making the story into a Velcro apron story or a metal board presentation. For an apron version, back the pieces with adhesive-backed Velcro but also glue them with Tacky glue. For a metal board story, use the adhesive-backed magnetic strips and Tacky glue.

Library Table Signs

1. Decide how to identify tables (by colors, numbers, letters or pictures). Instant Library Lessons uses colors.

2. Buy free-standing plastic picture frames (available in 8" x 10" or 5" x 7" from discount stores) for each table.

3. Create a different table identifier for each table in the appropriate size and place it in a frame.

4. Place a sign in the middle of each student table.

Great Rip Roar Read Report

1. Make copies of the Great Rip Roar Read Report on page 148.

2. Train the students to look for damage before leaving the library with a book.

3. If a student finds a book that needs repair he or she should fill out the report, then place the report in the damaged book and put them in the designated location.

Sample Room Layout

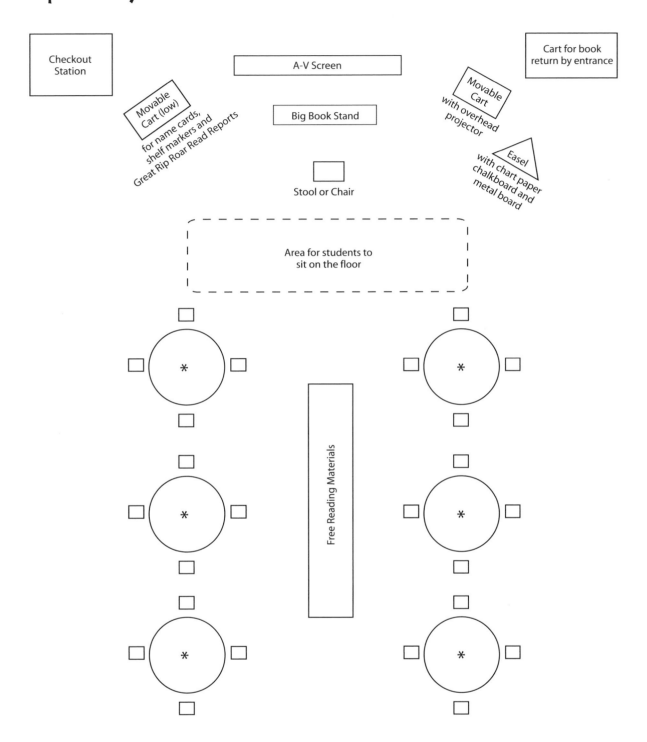

* table signs, baskets with colors, scissors, pencils and glue

One or more of the movable carts and/or big book stand should include storage for lesson materials for current lessons and lesson plan book.

❀ Lesson Learning Ideas ❀

The lesson learning ideas encompass six instructional strands. See page 6 for an explanation of each strand.

Library Skills

- Is familiar with a library setting

- Applies library manners

- Can identify the title, author and illustrator

- Can select books based on personal interest

- Comprehends library management skills

- Can follow circulation procedures

- Knows that materials in the library have a specific location and order

- Can identify the spine and spine label of a book

- Can locate a book in the easy fiction section by the author's last name

- Knows the spine label tells where a book is placed on the shelf

- Uses multiple resources to locate information

- Is developing a basic concept of the research process

- Can locate and identify the basic parts of a book

- Is familiar with basic reference books and their purpose

Literature Appreciation

- Participates in investigating character analysis

- Has had experience with various literary genres

- Has an understanding of the concept of artist and illustrator

- Has used fiction and nonfiction materials

- Has an initial understanding of the difference between fiction and nonfiction

- Understands the concept of variation in folktales

- Understands the concept of characters from works of fiction

- Knows the meaning of award-winning literature

- Has an understanding of how authors write books

- Understands and applies nonfiction reading techniques

- Is familiar with the fictional format of a cumulative story

Techniques of Learning

- Has established visual literacy skills

- Has experience in critical thinking questioning

- Has the opportunity to work in cooperative groups

- Has experience with compare and contrast questioning

- Understands and participates in brainstorming activities

- Is able to integrate cues from written and visual text

- Uses organizational formats for learning

- Can transfer learning experiences across multiple situations

- Attends to personal and/or team tasks outside of the whole group setting

- Participates in independent reading

- Takes an active role in recomposing visual and written information

Comprehension

- Has extended personal vocabulary

- Has enhanced personal sight word vocabulary

- Has experience in the comprehension strategy of retelling

- Has the opportunity to apply the comprehension strategy of story structure

- Has the opportunity to participate in experiences that support the acquisition of fluency

- Utilizes the comprehension strategy of prediction

- Is able to set a purpose for reading

- Is able to make connections with prior knowledge and experience

- Can recall, summarize and paraphrase what is listened to and viewed

- Is beginning to comprehend basic text structures

- Is developing the ability to generate appropriate questions

Writing Experiences

- Has participated in a variety of age-appropriate writing experiences

- Can create labels, notes and/or captions

- Is able to generate brief descriptions that use sensory details

- Responds to literature in a variety of written formats

- Uses prewriting strategies such as drawings, brainstorming and/or graphic organizers

- Imitates models of good writing

- Is able to transfer ideas into sentences with appropriate support

- Indicates an understanding of story structure necessary for narrative writing

- Participates in narrative writing experiences

- Participates in descriptive writing experiences

- Participates in expository writing experiences

- Has experience with examples of narrative writing and its uses

- Has experience with examples of descriptive writing and its uses

- Has experience with examples of expository writing and its uses

Oral Language

- Has taken part in storytelling and read aloud experiences

- Participates in audience participation storytelling

- Is able to listen to and comprehend a variety of oral presentation formats

- Is able to listen to and comprehend a variety of multimedia presentation formats

- Is developing the ability to respond to what is seen and heard

Focus on Frogs

Focus on Frogs • Lesson 1

Featured Books

How to Make a Paper Frog by Jan Pritchett. National Geographic School Publishing, 2004.

Teaches the use of shapes and following directions in creating an origami frog. ISBN 079224656X

I Took My Frog to the Library by Eric Kimmel. Puffin, 1990.

A young girl brings her pets to the library—with predictably disastrous results. ISBN 014050916X

Lesson Learning Ideas

Library Skills

- Is familiar with a library setting
- Applies library manners
- Comprehends library management skills
- Knows that materials in the library have a specific location and order

Techniques of Learning

- Is able to integrate cues from written and visual text
- Attends to personal and/or team tasks outside of the whole group setting

Writing Experiences

- Has experience with examples of expository writing and its uses

Oral Language

- Is developing the ability to respond to what is seen and heard

Materials

- *How to Make a Paper Frog* by Jan Pritchett (see Ordering Information, page 149)
- *I Took My Frog to the Library* by Eric Kimmel
- stuffed animals listed in Lesson Plan, step 1 (see Ordering Information, page 149)

- take-home picture (page 19)

- shelf marker

- construction paper

- scissors

- glue

- pencils

- crayons

Before Class

1. Make a copy of the take-home picture for each student.

2. Gather and prepare the materials needed for the paper frog activity—see *How to Make a Paper Frog* for instructions.

3. Gather stuffed animals for the story.

Lesson Plan

1. Present *I Took My Frog to the Library*. Use beanie baby animals for the frog, snake, giraffe, pelican, hen and hyena. If a hyena is not available, you can substitute a parrot without altering the story content. A large elephant is also needed to complete the story.

2. This story is a good way to introduce the rules and important places in a library. Alter it to fit the individual needs of your library. After the story, play I Spy. For example, I spy the frog. Where is the frog? The frog is on the librarian's desk.

3. Introduce *How to Make a Paper Frog*. As you read aloud, demonstrate each step.

4. Provide each student with the necessary materials. Read through the book again, this time with the students following the instructions to create their own frog.

5. Share that the students will soon select books from the shelves to check out. In order to be able to take books from the shelves, they need to know about shelf markers. Briefly demonstrate how a shelf marker is used in a library.

6. Give each student a take-home picture to color based on today's story and experience in the library.

Today in the library we read...
I Took My Frog to the Library
by Eric Kimmel

Focus on Frogs · Lesson 2

Featured Books

The Wide-Mouthed Frog by Keith Faulkner. Dial, 1996.

A wide-mouthed frog is interested in what other animals eat—until he meets a creature who eats only wide-mouthed frogs. ISBN 0803718756

The Edible Pyramid by Loreen Leedy. Holiday House, 1994.

Uses the U.S. Department of Agriculture's food guide pyramid to show the healthy way to eat, including how many daily servings are recommended from each food group. ISBN 0823411265

Lesson Learning Ideas

Library Skills

- Comprehends library management skills
- Knows that materials in the library have a specific location and order

Literature Appreciation

- Has used fiction and nonfiction materials
- Has an initial understanding of the difference between fiction and nonfiction

Techniques of Learning

- Has experience with compare and contrast questioning
- Uses organizational formats for learning

Comprehension

- Is able to make connections with prior knowledge and experience

Materials

- *The Edible Pyramid* by Loreen Leedy
- *The Wide-Mouthed Frog* by Keith Faulkner
- materials for creating shelf markers—see Before Class
- The Food Pyramid worksheet (page 22)
- My Favorite Food worksheet (page 23)

Before Class

1. Gather materials for students to use to create shelf markers. Cut poster board into 8″ x 3″ strips. You can also use materials like Styrofoam meat trays (cut into strips) or paint stir sticks. Make crayons, markers, colored paper, glue, scissors and/or stickers available to the students.

2. Enlarge the Food Pyramid worksheet so it is poster size, or draw it on a board.

3. Copy enough My Favorite Food worksheets for each student.

Lesson Plan

1. Give each student a My Favorite Food worksheet. Ask the students to draw a picture showing something they like to eat. As they draw, circulate around the room and print the name of what they are drawing on each picture.

2. When the students are finished, display the Food Pyramid and introduce the food groups by reading aloud *The Edible Pyramid*. Use a few of the students' pictures to discuss which foods go in which groups. Have the students place their pictures in the correct group. Discuss where most of the favorite foods appear.

3. Tell the children you are going to share a story about what a frog and some other animals eat. Read *The Wide-Mouthed Frog* aloud using the pop-up book.

4. Reinforce the idea of shelf markers from lesson 1. Show the picture of the frog on the first page of *The Wide-Mouthed Frog*. Bring the students' attention to how the frog sticks out its tongue to get what it wants. Ask students how a frog's tongue is like a shelf marker and how it is different. Show students again how a shelf marker is used and why it is important.

5. Provide students with materials to decorate shelf markers.

The Food Pyramid

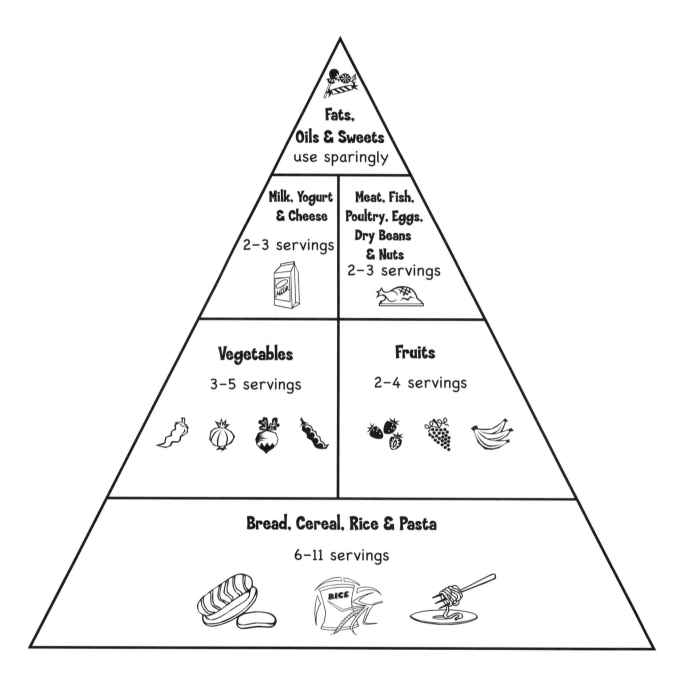

Fats,
Oils & Sweets
use sparingly

Milk, Yogurt
& Cheese

2–3 servings

Meat, Fish,
Poultry, Eggs,
Dry Beans
& Nuts
2–3 servings

Vegetables

3–5 servings

Fruits

2–4 servings

Bread, Cereal, Rice & Pasta

6–11 servings

My Favorite Food

Draw a picture of your favorite food on the plate.

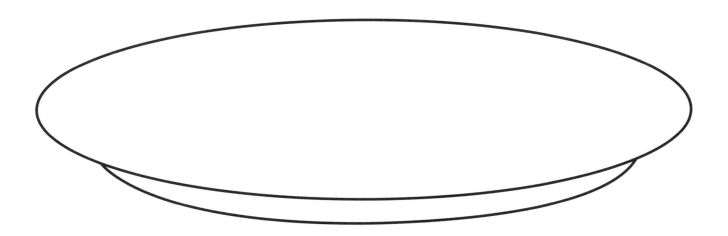

My favorite food is _____.

Focus on Frogs • Lesson 3

Featured Book

Time for Bed, the Babysitter Said by Peggy Perry Anderson.
Houghton Mifflin, 1987.

Not even his babysitter's most strenuous efforts can convince Joe the frog to
go to bed. ISBN 0395418518

Lesson Learning Ideas

Library Skills

- Knows that materials in the library have a specific location and order

- Can identify the spine and spine label of a book

- Knows the spine label tells where a book is placed on the shelf

Techniques of Learning

- Has the opportunity to work in cooperative groups

- Attends to personal and/or team tasks outside of the whole group setting

Comprehension

- Utilizes the comprehension strategy of prediction

- Is able to make connections with prior knowledge and experience

Writing Experiences

- Participates in expository writing experiences

- Imitates models of good writing

- Has participated in a variety of age-appropriate writing experiences

- Is able to transfer ideas into sentences with appropriate support

Materials

- *Time for Bed, the Babysitter Said* by Peggy Perry Anderson

- frog stickers (available at school supply stores)

- index cards in various colors

- Stimulate Prior Knowledge Visual—Connection Stems (page 26)

Before Class

1. Purchase double sets of frog stickers. Use index cards in different colors to create decks of cards. Each deck should have pairs of cards featuring the same frog stickers. If time permits, laminate the cards before they are used.

2. Make a transparency of the Stimulate Prior Knowledge Visual.

Lesson Plan

1. Show the cover of *Time for Bed, the Babysitter Said* and read aloud the title and author. Ask the students to brainstorm what they think the story is about. Use the headings shown in the Stimulate Prior Knowledge Visual to ask the students: How might this book be like something that happened in your life? How might this book be like something that happened in someone else's life? How might this book be like other books you have read/heard?

2. Read the story aloud, allowing ample time with the illustrations.

3. Explain to the children that if books could talk they might say: "Thank you for using shelf markers so I can get back to my home on the shelf." In addition, they might say: "Please be careful of biting books."

4. Share with students what and where a spine is on a book. Instruct the children to feel their own spine. Then tell them to pretend that the other side of the book (where the pages are) is a book's mouth. Show how a book opens and closes like a mouth. Tell the children that when they put a book back on the shelf they should always hold it by its backbone/spine and not its mouth—that way they won't have to worry about biting books.

5. To extend the story idea of saying "please" and "thank you," students can play a frog version of Go Fish called "Go Jump in the Pond." Explain the rules for Go Fish. Remind the students to say please and thank you each time they take a turn.

6. After the children play the card game, bring them back into the group. Remind them of the book *How to Make a Paper Frog*. Explain that this book gave directions for something. As a group try to create a list of instructions for playing Go Jump in the Pond.

Connection Stems

book → me

book → book

book → world

Focus on Frogs • Lesson 4

Featured Book

The Complete Grimm's Fairy Tales. Pantheon Books, 1972.

A collection of 210 traditional tales by the brothers Grimm, with accompanying explanatory and historical material. ISBN 0394709306

Lesson Learning Ideas

Library Skills

- Can select books based on personal interest

- Comprehends library management skills

- Can follow circulation procedures

- Knows that materials in the library have a specific location and order

- Can locate and identify the basic parts of a book

Literature Appreciation

- Understands the concept of variation in folktales

Techniques of Learning

- Has the opportunity to work in cooperative groups

- Has experience with compare and contrast questioning

- Attends to personal and/or team tasks outside of the whole group setting

Materials

- *The Complete Grimm's Fairy Tales*

- *Same-Different Fairy Tales* by Spencer Kagan (see Ordering Information, page 149)

- all of the versions of "The Frog Prince" from your collection

Before Class

1. Copy, mount and laminate the pictures for the frog prince activity from *Same-Different Fairy Tales*. It is helpful to mount all of the No. 1 pictures on one color of construction paper and all of the No. 2 pictures on a different color.

2. Copy the cover and title page from each frog prince book in your collection. Make concentration game folders by gathering enough file folders to have one for each item copied. In large print on the outside of each folder number the folders from one to ten (use as many folders as are needed to include all of the book covers and title pages). After the folders have been laminated, open them up and cut a small slit near the top of the inside of the folder. Place a paper clip through the slit to hold the copy in place.

Lesson Plan

1. Tell the old fairy tale often called "The Frog Prince." Use a version based on "The Frog-King, or Iron Henry" found in *The Complete Grimm's Fairy Tales*. **Note:** It might be prudent to vary the ending so that the young girl has a change of heart instead of throwing the frog against the wall.

2. Show the students other versions of "The Frog Prince." For example: *The Horned Toad Prince* by Jackie Hopkins, *The Frog Princess* by Rosalind Allchin and *The Frog Principal* by Stephanie Calmenson. Explain that in the coming weeks they are going to read and compare some of the other versions of this story. (Additional versions include: *A Frog Prince* by Alix Berenzy, *The Frog Prince—Continued* by Jon Scieszka, *The Prong Frince* by C. Drew Lamm and *The Princess and the Frog* by Will Eisner.)

3. Share the cover of one of the books and have the students name each part of the cover. Then share the title page. Compare the information on the cover with what is found on the title page.

4. Play a game of concentration in which the students match the cover of a book with its title page.

5. Have the students participate in a Same-Different Activity (see below) while a few students check out. Having only a few students at the shelf at a time allows for better monitoring of the use of shelf markers and other needs.

Directions for Same-Different Activity

Divide the students into pairs. Give each pair of students the two different pictures from the same-different activity. Have the children look at the pictures side by side. Explain that there are 20 things that are different in the two pictures. Ask the children to work with their partners to look for the differences. Next, explain that there are also 20 things that are alike about the two pictures. Model some examples as this is the harder concept to grasp.

Focus on Frogs • Lesson 5

Featured Book

The Frog Principal by Stephanie Calmenson. Scholastic, 2001.

When Marty Q. Marvel the magician turns Mr. Bundy into a frog, the students of PS 88 don't know what to do with their new administrator. It's not always easy having a slimy, green-skinned amphibian for a principal. ISBN 0590370707

Lesson Learning Ideas

Literature Appreciation

- Understands the concept of variation in folktales

Techniques of Learning

- Has experience in critical thinking questioning

- Has experience with compare and contrast questioning

- Uses organizational formats for learning

Comprehension

- Is developing the ability to generate appropriate questions

- Can recall, summarize and paraphrase what is listened to and viewed

Writing Experiences

- Responds to literature in a variety of written formats

Oral Language

- Has taken part in storytelling and read aloud experiences

- Is developing the ability to respond to what is seen and heard

Materials

- *The Frog Principal* by Stephanie Calmenson

- Frog Prince Book Questions visual (page 31)

- Question Stems visual (page 32)

Before Class

1. Prepare the Question Stems visual for display. Make a transparency, individual cards or a chart so that the whole class can view them at one time.

2. Decide how to share the Frog Prince Book Questions visual with the students. The questions can be displayed on a chart, chalkboard or transparency. This same visual will be used in several lessons.

Lesson Plan

1. Share *The Frog Principal* as a follow-me read aloud. Provide one copy of the book for every two to three students. Have the students follow along in their copy as you read the story.

2. Ask the students to answer the Frog Prince Book Questions visual. Lead a discussion comparing the original version of "The Frog Prince" with today's story. Save the answers from today for the upcoming lessons.

3. Share that good readers ask themselves questions as they read to help check their understanding. Display the Question Stems visual and offer the icons so that all of the students can read the stems independently. Share examples of how to create questions using these stems. Examples might include: **What did** Marty Q. Marvel turn Mr. Bundy into? or **When did** Mr. Bundy change back into a man? Working with one stem pair at a time, ask the students to come up with their own questions about the story. Record the student questions.

Frog Prince Book Questions

Questions	The Frog Prince	The Frog Principal	The Horned Toad Prince	The Frog Princess	The Frog Princess?
Where does the story happen?					
Use two or three words to describe the princess.					
What part does the ball play in the story?					
Use two or three words to describe the frog.					
What does magic have to do with the story?					
What problems does the frog have in the story?					
What happens at the end of the story?					

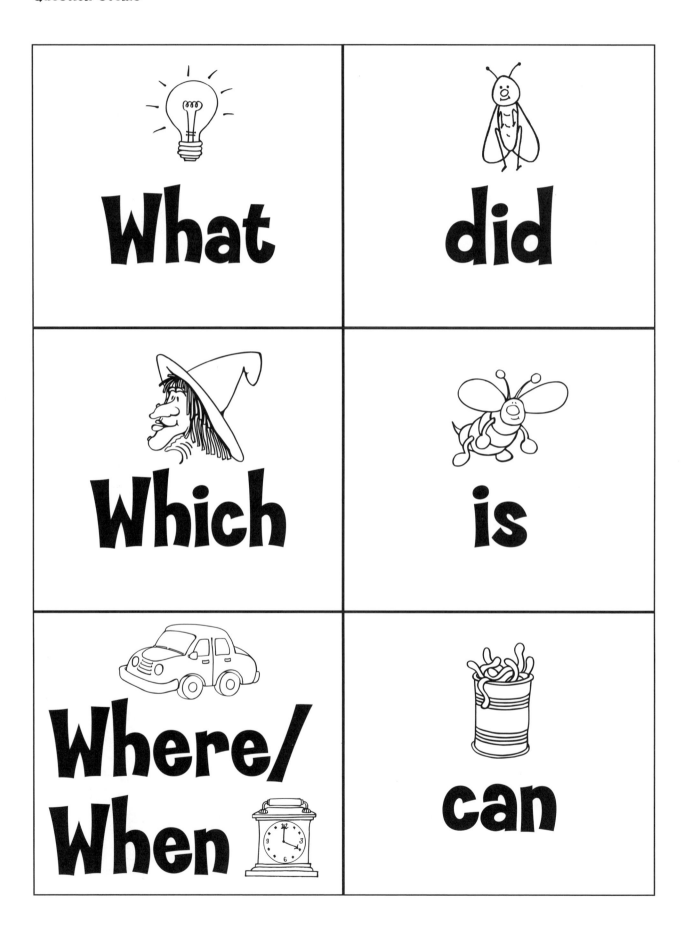

What

did

Which

is

Where/ When

can

Focus on Frogs • Lesson 6

Featured Book

The Horned Toad Prince by Jackie Mims Hopkins. Peachtree Publishers, 2000.

In this retelling of "The Frog Prince," a spunky cowgirl loses her new sombrero and is helped by a horned toad on the understanding that she will do three small favors for him in return. ISBN 1561451959

Lesson Learning Ideas

Literature Appreciation

- Understands the concept of variation in folktales

Techniques of Learning

- Has experience in critical thinking questioning

- Has experience with compare and contrast questioning

- Is able to integrate cues from written and visual text

- Takes an active role in recomposing visual and written information

- Uses organizational formats for learning

Comprehension

- Has experience in the comprehension strategy of retelling

- Can recall, summarize and paraphrase what is listened to and viewed

Oral Language

- Is developing the ability to respond to what is seen and heard

Materials

- *The Horned Toad Prince* by Jackie Mims Hopkins

- Frog Prince Book Questions visual from previous lesson

- Venn Diagram Outlines (page 35)

Before Class

1. Practice the Spanish words that are listed on the back inside cover of the book or find someone who speaks Spanish to read the words as they occur in the story.

2. Reproduce the Venn Diagrams Outlines for use with the class.

Lesson Plan

1. Read aloud *The Horned Toad Prince*. Share the Spanish words in the story with the students.

2. Direct the children's attention to the Frog Prince Book Questions from the last lesson. Have the children answer the questions based on today's story. As with the princess question from *The Frog Principal*, sometimes the question does not apply to a particular book.

3. Present the Venn Diagram Outlines and explain a Venn diagram's uses. Ask the children to look for the items that are the same in both *The Frog Principal* and *The Horned Toad Prince*. Use the questions as a starting place, but don't limit the comparison to the questions. Similarities might include that both are based on "The Frog Prince" fairy tale, are picture books, teach a lesson about keeping promises, etc.

4. If the students grasp the concept of a Venn diagram, try a three-way comparison. Use the original story and the two variations presented thus far. Find the information on the chart before trying to recompose it onto the Venn diagram.

Venn Diagram Outlines

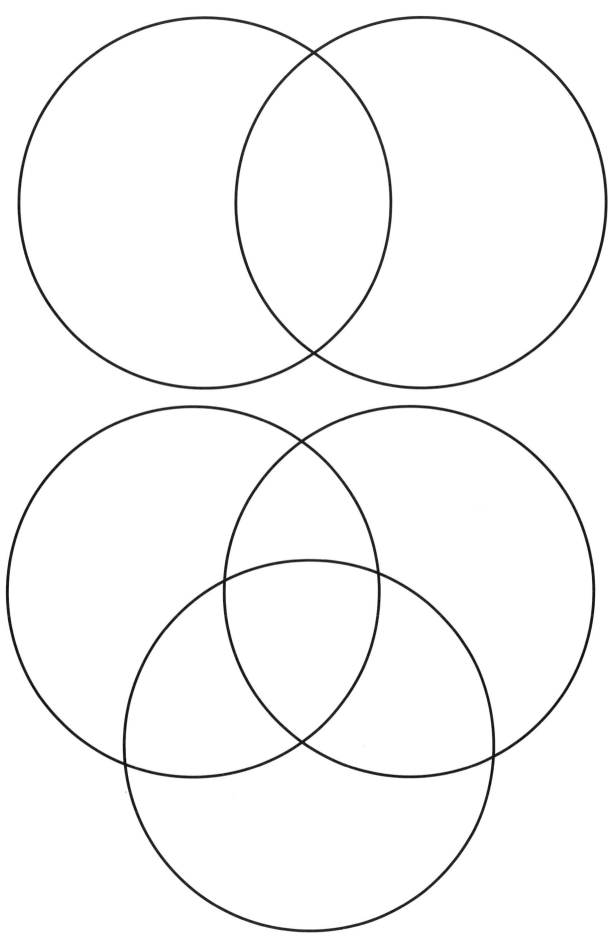

Focus on Frogs • Lesson 7

Featured Books

The Frog Princess **by Rosalind Allchin. Kids Can Press, 2001.**

Frog dreams constantly about how wonderful it would be to be a princess, but when she is given an opportunity to try out the role for a day, she learns that life as a member of the royal family is much more stressful than she imagined. ISBN 1553375262

The Frog Princess? **by Pamela Mann. Mantra Publishing, 1995.**

A lonely, ugly frog is approached, and misunderstood, by many animals until one day a handsome prince understands why she croaks "Reddit! Reddit!" ISBN 185269324X

Lesson Learning Ideas

Library Skills

* Can identify title, author and illustrator

Literature Appreciation

* Participates in investigating character analysis

* Understands the concept of variation in folktales

* Understands the concept of characters from works of fiction

Techniques of Learning

* Has experience in critical thinking questioning

* Has experience with compare and contrast questioning

* Can transfer learning experiences across multiple situations

* Takes an active role in recomposing visual and written information

Comprehension

* Has the opportunity to apply the comprehension strategy of story structure

* Has experience in the comprehension strategy of retelling

Writing Experiences

* Responds to literature in a variety of written formats

- Imitates models of good writing

- Participates in narrative writing experiences

- Has experience with examples of narrative writing and its uses

Materials

- *The Frog Princess* by Rosalind Allchin

- *The Frog Princess?* by Pamela Mann

- Frog Prince Book Questions visual from the previous lessons

- art paper and crayons

Before Class

Gather copies of "Black Beauty," "Chicken Little" and "Puss in Boots" in single book format.

Lesson Plan

1. If possible, provide enough copies of *The Frog Princess* by Allchin so there is one book for every two or three students. Read the story aloud as the students follow along in their copies of the book.

2. Focus the students' attention on the Frog Prince Book Questions. Have the students help fill in the answers based on the story. The one thing that has been different in each version is the location. Have the children create a list of other locations to which this story could be transferred. Lead a discussion of how the story might be different if the location was different.

3. Allow the students to select one location for a new frog prince story and draw a picture for the cover of the book. Have them create a title for their version. When the students finish their pictures, have them share the pictures in small groups or with the whole class.

4. Introduce *The Frog Princess?* by Mann. Share that in this story the setting is similar but the frog princess character is different. Read the story aloud.

5. After the story, continue talking about characters. In this story there were three animal characters from other children's stories. Ask the students to list the animals and the story clues they gave. Then show copies of "Black Beauty," "Chicken Little" and "Puss in Boots." These may not be stories the children know. Have the students come up with three animal characters from stories they all easily recognize. Then have them insert the character and a story clue into the story frame.

Focus on Frogs · Lesson 8

Featured Book

The Caterpillar and the Polliwog by Jack Kent. Simon & Schuster, 1982.
Impressed by the proud caterpillar's boast that she will turn into a butterfly when she grows up, a polliwog determines to watch the caterpillar very carefully and learn how to turn into a butterfly herself. ISBN 0671662813

Lesson Learning Ideas

Techniques of Learning

- Has established visual literacy skills

- Has experience in critical thinking questioning

- Is able to integrate cues from written and visual text

- Uses organizational formats for learning

- Attends to personal and/or team tasks outside of the whole group setting

- Takes an active role in recomposing visual and written information

Comprehension

- Utilizes the comprehension strategy of prediction

- Is able to set a purpose for reading

Oral Language

- Is developing the ability to respond to what is seen and heard

Materials

- *The Caterpillar and the Polliwog* by Jack Kent book and video (see Ordering Information, page 149)

- Frog Glyph worksheet (page 40)

- several completed frog glyphs as examples

Before Class

1. Gather materials for the glyph activity. Each student will need a copy of the frog and lily pad pictures from 41–42. In addition, they will need scissors, glue, crayons and construction paper.

2. Make a transparency of the glyph.

3. Create several completed glyphs as examples.

Lesson Plan

1. Show the cover of *The Caterpillar and the Polliwog* and read the title. Ask the students if they can figure out what a polliwog is from the cover illustration.

2. Show the seven-minute video of *The Caterpillar and the Polliwog.*

3. Introduce the concept of a glyph. It is based on Egyptian writing called *hieroglyphics* or picture writing. Tell the students that they are going to create their own *glyphs,* or pictures, which can be read.

4. Walk through the criteria for the glyph from page 40 and use your examples to illustrate how each criterion is shown. Ask the students to think about how they would show their answer on their glyph. For example, while you discuss the frog color, students may want to color in just a little of their frog to help them remember what color they are going to use. If students have not had experiences constructing glyphs they will most likely only finish construction during one class. If students have had experience, you will probably have time for construction and analyzing.

5. To analyze the glyphs, post them so they can all be viewed at one time. Ask questions involving one criterion. For example: How many people would like to swim like a frog? How did you figure out your answer? Once students can read with one criterion move to two criteria. For example: How many people who would like to swim like a frog have ever held a frog?

Frog Glyph

Name: _____

Date: _____

Frog Color

Green	Brown	Red
If you have ever held a frog in your hand	If you would like to hold a frog	If you would not like to hold a frog

Lily Pad

Frog Sitting in the Water	Frog Sitting on the Lily Pad
If you wish you could swim like a frog	If you wish you could jump like a frog

Crown

Without a Crown	With a Crown
If you like true books about frogs like the book _____	If you like make-believe books about frogs like the book _____

Frog Glyph Pictures

Photocopy to desired size.

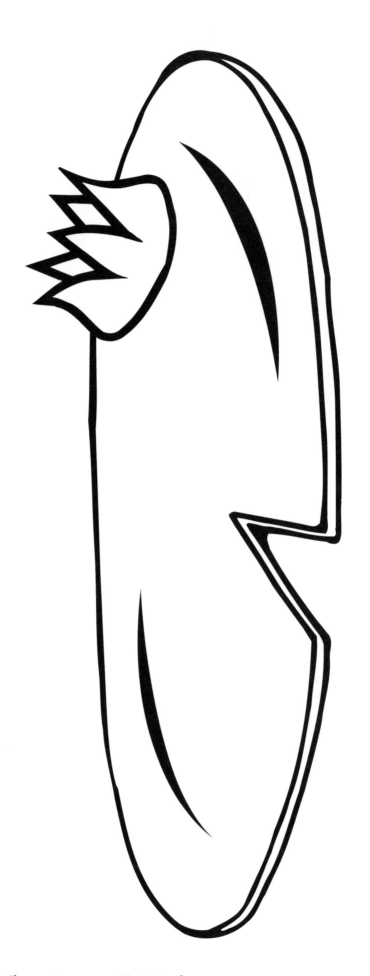

Focus on Frogs • Lesson 9

Featured Books

The Mysterious Tadpole by Steven Kellogg. Dial, 2002.

It soon becomes clear that Louis's pet tadpole is not turning into an ordinary frog. (For the twenty-fifth anniversary edition Kellogg offers a somewhat expanded version of the story along with new artwork.) ISBN 0803727887 (Giant Edition ISBN 0140545697)

Talking with Artists: Volume 1 by Pat Cummings. Simon & Schuster, 1992.

Fourteen distinguished picture book artists talk about their early art experiences, answer questions most frequently asked by children and offer encouragement to those who would like to become artists. ISBN 0027242455

Lesson Learning Ideas

Library Skills

- Is developing a basic concept of the research process

- Uses multiple resources to locate information

- Is familiar with basic reference books and their purpose

Literature Appreciation

- Has an understanding of the concept of artist and illustrator

- Has an understanding of how authors write books

- Has used fiction and nonfiction materials

Comprehension

- Can recall, summarize and paraphrase what is listened to and viewed

Writing Experiences

- Uses prewriting strategies such as drawings, brainstorming and/or graphic organizers

Materials

- *The Mysterious Tadpole* by Steven Kellogg big book or video (see Ordering Information, page 149)

- other books written and/or illustrated by Steven Kellogg

- *Trumpet Video Visits Steven Kellogg* (see Ordering Information, page 149)

- art materials for students

- *Talking with Artists: Volume 1* by Pat Cummings

Before Class

Gather all the books written or illustrated by Steven Kellogg from your library collection.

Lesson Plan

1. Ask the students what a baby that grows into a frog is called. Remind them of *The Caterpillar and the Polliwog.* If the students don't remember, prompt them that the answer is a tadpole. Explain that today's story is about a mysterious tadpole, a tadpole like no other tadpole. Share the story from the nine-minute video of *The Mysterious Tadpole.*

2. Show the front cover of the book. Ask the children who the author is. Then ask who the illustrator is. Have the students explain why they think their answer is right.

3. Explain that Steven Kellogg has written and illustrated more than 25 books. In addition, he has illustrated more than 85 books. Share the 17-minute *Trumpet Video Visits Steven Kellogg.*

4. Begin a class list of Steven Kellogg books. See how many titles the children can find. The list can be divided into books written and illustrated and books just illustrated. Help the students investigate sources to use in finding this information.

5. Introduce *Talking with Artists.* Share the information about Steven Kellogg. Then ask students to help make a list of facts about Kellogg and his writing. When the students have developed a list give each student a piece of paper. Ask the children to write down one fact from the list, then illustrate the information. Create a display of these pictures under the heading "Did You Know?"

Focus on Frogs • Lesson 10

Featured Book

Frog by Angela Royston. Heinemann Library, 2000.

An introduction to the life cycle of a frog from the time it is a tiny egg until it is two years old. ISBN 1575725363

Lesson Learning Ideas

Library Skills

- Uses multiple resources to locate information
- Is developing a basic concept of the research process

Literature Appreciation

- Has used fiction and nonfiction materials
- Has an initial understanding of the difference between fiction and nonfiction
- Understands and applies nonfiction reading techniques

Techniques of Learning

- Has established visual literacy skills
- Has the opportunity to work in cooperative groups
- Is able to integrate cues from written and visual text
- Uses organizational formats for learning
- Attends to personal and/or team tasks outside of the whole group setting
- Takes an active role in recomposing visual and written information

Comprehension

- Has extended personal vocabulary
- Has experience in the comprehension strategy of retelling
- Can recall, summarize and paraphrase what is listened to and viewed
- Is beginning to comprehend basic text features

Writing Experience

- Can create labels, notes and/or captions
- Responds to literature in a variety of written formats

Oral Language

- Is developing the ability to respond to what is seen and heard

Materials

- *Frog* by Angela Royston big book (see Ordering Information, page 149)
- Cyclical Flow Diagram visual (page 47)
- frog metamorphosis model (see Ordering Information, page 149)
- *The Mysterious Tadpole* by Steven Kellogg
- *The Caterpillar and the Polliwog* by Jack Kent
- art paper and crayons

Before Class

1. Make several copies of the diagram for students to use and at least one for class use.

2. Gather multiple copies of the Kellogg and Kent books for small group work.

Lesson Plan

1. Read aloud *Frog*. Direct the students to the life cycle picture on pages 28 and 29 and the diagram at the bottom of each page. Discuss how the tadpole changes through each phase. For additional information introduce the frog metamorphosis model. Have the students put them in order and name each representation.

3. Introduce the Cyclical Flow Diagram. As a class, recompose the book representation into a cyclical flow diagram. Share that "cyclical flow diagrams are best suited to describing continuous renewable processes. Topics that tend to lend themselves to these diagrams include natural processes, repetitive processes in technology or environmental topics." (From *I See What You Mean: Children at Work with Visual Information* by Steve Moline. Stenhouse Publishers, 1996.)

4. Return to *The Caterpillar and the Polliwog* and *The Mysterious Tadpole*. Use the pictures in each book and walk through the life cycle for the polliwog and for Alphonse. Use something to mark each picture that is one phase of a life cycle presentation.

5. Divide the children into groups. Assign one group to use *The Caterpillar and the Polliwog* and one to use *The Mysterious Tadpole*. To allow for greater involvement, make groups smaller by having more than one work on creating a diagram based on a given book. Instruct each group to construct their own life cycle picture based on their book. Encourage each group member to draw at least one phase. Provide the groups with a cyclical flow diagram. Allow time for the students to share their life cycle representations.

Cyclical Flow Diagram

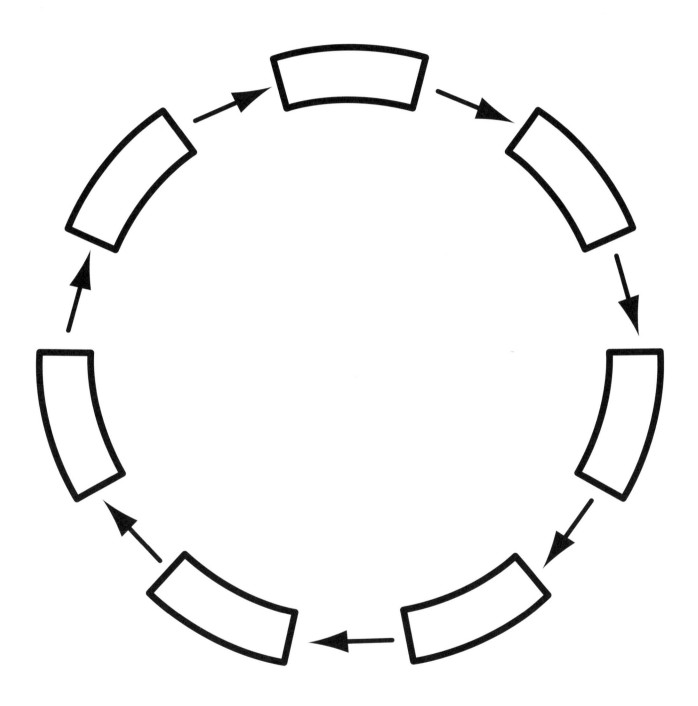

Focus on Frogs • Lesson 11

Featured Book

Frog by Angela Royston. Heinemann Library, 2000.

An introduction to the life cycle of a frog from the time it is a tiny egg until it is two years old. ISBN 1575725363

Lesson Learning Ideas

Library Skills

- Uses multiple resources to locate information

Literature Appreciation

- Understands and applies nonfiction reading techniques

Techniques of Learning

- Uses organizational formats for learning

- Takes an active role in recomposing visual and written information

Comprehension

- Is beginning to comprehend basic text structures

Materials

- Data Bank form (page 50)

- age-appropriate nonfiction books and magazines on frogs

- Post-it notes or easy release painters' tape

- *Frog* by Angela Royston

- art paper and crayons

Before Class

Create a class Data Bank form for each first grade class.

Lesson Plan

1. Direct the students' attention to the last page in *Frog*. Explain the "More Books to Read" section and why it is included.

2. Explain that the students will search for information about frogs in other books. Introduce the Data Bank form by going over the categories and explaining the icons; the icons help students who can't read the words, for example, everything a person "has" goes in a suitcase when they travel. Share some or all of the facts about frogs from *Frog* using the Fact File on page 30. Let students select where to include the facts on the Data Bank worksheet.

3. Provide books and magazines for students to look at and/or read. Model how students can locate and mark information in the text or pictures that will be helpful for the Data Bank. As the children "read," have them use Post-it notes or painters' tape to mark the location of information they think will fit in the Data Bank.

4. Reassemble the class and work on filling in the Data Bank form. Words and/or pictures can be used to fill in the information. If there are categories that need more information redirect students back to the materials to locate what is needed.

5. Divide the students into five groups. Assign each group one of the categories from the Data Bank. Encourage everyone to construct a picture or pictures that illustrate the information/facts from their category of the Data Bank worksheet.

6. Explain that the Data Bank information will be saved for the next class when the students will help write a report about frogs.

Suggested Nonfiction Books

- *Fabulous Frogs* by Linda Glaser. Millbrook Press, 1999. (RL 1.7)

- *Frogs* by Susan Canizares. Scholastic, 1998. (RL 1.3)

- *Frogs* by Gail Smith-Saunders. Capstone Press, 1998. (RL 1.3)

- *From Tadpole to Frog* by Jan Kottke. Scholastic Library Publishing, 2000. (RL 1.7)

- *From Tadpole to Frog* by Kathleen W. Zoehfeld. Scholastic, 2002. (RL 1.5)

- *How a Frog Grows* by Celia Benton. Compass Point Books, 2004. (RL 0.9)

- *I Can Read About Frogs and Toads* by Ellen Schultz. Troll Communications, 1979. (RL 2.0)

- *Jumpy, Green, and Croaky* by Moira Butterfield. Steck-Vaughn, 1998. (RL 1.5)

- *Life as a Frog* by Victoria Parker. Raintree Publishers, 2004. (RL 1.3)

- *Rainforest Colors* by Susan Canizares. Scholastic, 1998. (RL 1.0)

- *Red-eyed Tree Frogs* by John Netherton. Lerner Publishing Group, 2000. (RL 1.8)

- *Tree Frogs* by Marfe F. Delano. National Geographic Society, 2000. (RL 0.3)

- *Where do Frogs Come From?* by Alex Vern. Harcourt, 2003. (RL 1.7)

Data Bank for a _____

Lives:

1. _____
2. _____
3. _____

Eats:

1. _____
2. _____
3. _____

Looks like:

1. _____
2. _____
3. _____

Has:

1. _____
2. _____
3. _____

Does:

1. _____
2. _____
3. _____

Data Bank form adapted with permission from *Research Reports to Knock Your Teacher's Socks Off!* by Nancy Polette. Pieces of Learning, 1997.

Featured Book

No featured materials are needed for this lesson.

Lesson Learning Ideas

Library Skills

- Uses multiple resources to locate information

- Is developing a basic concept of the research process

- Can locate and identify the basic parts of a book

Literature Appreciation

- Has used fiction and nonfiction materials

Techniques of Learning

- Is able to integrate cues from written and visual text

- Uses organizational formats for learning

- Takes an active role in recomposing visual and written information

Writing Experiences

- Has participated in a variety of age-appropriate writing experiences

- Responds to literature in a variety of written formats

- Uses prewriting strategies such as drawings, brainstorming and/or graphic organizers

- Imitates models of good writing

- Participates in expository writing experiences

Oral Language

- Is developing the ability to respond to what is seen and heard

Materials

- Data Bank form from Lesson 11

- Writing Frame for Frogs worksheet (page 53)

- age-appropriate nonfiction books and magazines on frogs used in Lesson 11
- art paper and crayons

Before Class

1. Create a class-size copy of the writing frame and individual student-size copies.

2. Post the appropriate class Data Bank information.

Lesson Plan

1. Review the Data Bank information from Lesson 11 with the students.

2. Introduce the Writing Frame for Frogs worksheet. Read through it for the class. Explain that the class is going to write a frog report together. Later, students can choose to create their own if they want and if time permits.

3. Follow the frame section by section to decide where to find the information on the Data Bank. Have the students select what will be included. Write the information on the class report.

4. Have the students fill in their own forms as the class works and then illustrate the finished product. Another option is to have the students watch as you fill in the frame, and then fill in their own frame as they see fit. Be sure to allow time for the students to illustrate what they have done.

5. Review the components of a book cover and title page with the students. Then allow time for them to create a cover and title page for the report as though it was a book.

Writing Frame for Frogs

I am a frog. Come to my home in _____

_____.

I am a frog. Hear me _____.

See my _____.

See my _____.

I am a frog. Watch me _____.

Watch me _____.

I am a frog, hear me, see me, but watch out, I may be watching you.

Writing Frame worksheet adapted with permission from *Research Reports to Knock Your Teacher's Socks Off!*
by Nancy Polette. Pieces of Learning, 1997.

Quilt Me a Story

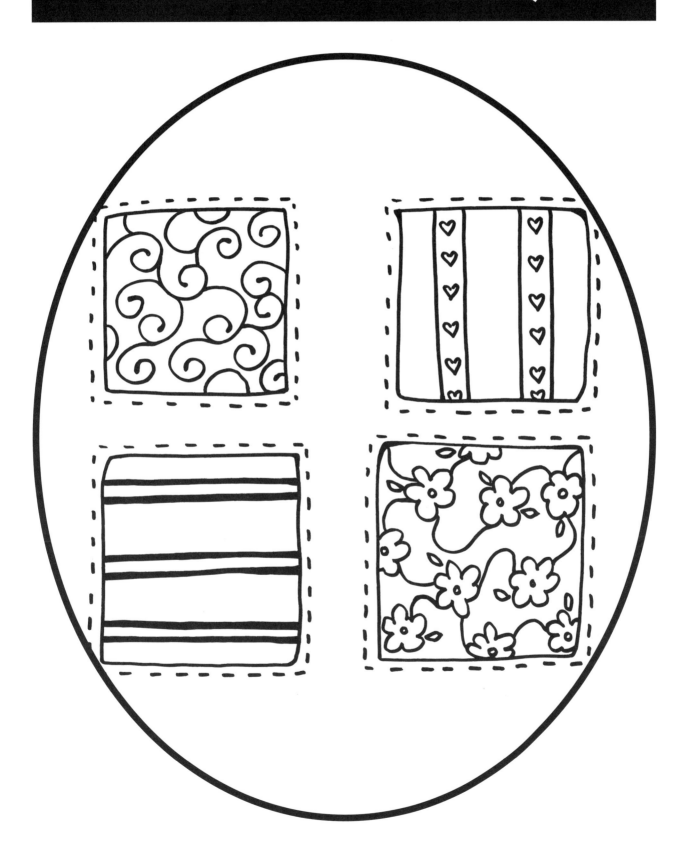

Quilt Me a Story • Lesson 1

Featured Book

Joseph Had a Little Overcoat by Simms Taback. Viking, 1999.

A very old overcoat is recycled numerous times into a variety of garments. ISBN 0670878553

Lesson Learning Ideas

Literature Appreciation

- Has had experience with various literary genres

- Knows the meaning of award-winning literature

- Has an understanding of how authors write books

Techniques of Learning

- Attends to personal and/or team tasks outside the whole group setting

Comprehension

- Has the opportunity to participate in experiences that support the acquisition of fluency

- Has experience in the comprehension strategy of retelling

- Can recall, summarize and paraphrase what is listened to and viewed

Oral Language

- Has taken part in storytelling and read aloud experiences

Materials

- trunk or box with examples of the three different kinds of quilts

- *Joseph Had a Little Overcoat* by Simms Taback

- *Joseph Had a Little Overcoat* 11-minute video (see Ordering Information, page 149)

- books based on songs from your library collection

- *Joseph Had a Little Overcoat* Literature Pictures (pages 59–60)

- crayons

- metal board and/or Velcro board

Before Class

1. Make enough copies of the *Joseph Had a Little Overcoat* Literature Pictures for each student and several sets for the free reading section. See the Literature Picture directions on page 10. Be sure to enlarge the picture of the man and enlarge the clothes in the same proportion. As the story progresses add or remove the clothing items (which have been backed with tape) in time with the story action.

2. Gather books based on children's songs from your collection.

3. Prepare a trunk or box with at least three examples of the different types of quilts inside.

Lesson Plan

1. Take a patchwork quilt out of the trunk and explain that it is the most common kind of quilt. People simply took old pieces of cloth from worn-out clothes and other scraps of material, cut them into squares and pieced them together. Take out a quilt made with a quilt pattern. Explain that people have developed thousands of quilt patterns or pictures. Finally show an appliqué quilt. These are often the most difficult to make and are sometimes made as works of art instead of blankets to sleep under. Tell the students that the books in this unit include stories about each of these three kinds of quilts.

2. Share that today's story is not about a quilt, but it is a good story to start this unit.

3. Share *Joseph Had a Little Overcoat* using any of the methods available. Have the students discuss why they think this book was chosen to start a unit on quilt stories.

4. Share the author information from the back of the book. If you have time, discuss award-winning books. The book also provides an insight into the struggles that authors and illustrators have with their work.

5. Tell the students about the song the book is based on (see the information in the back of the book). Provide other books based on songs for students to enjoy during free reading time. Explain that the books will be available for check out during the next class session.

6. Introduce metal boards and/or Velcro boards from the free reading area. Give each student his or her own copy of the Literature Pictures and provide coloring time. Show the students the copies of *Joseph Had a Little Overcoat* in the free reading area.

Suggested Books Based on Songs

- *A-Hunting We Will Go* by Steven Kellogg. William Morrow & Co., 1998.
- *Bingo* by Rosemary Wells. Scholastic, 1999.
- *Down by the Station* by Will Hillenbrand. Harcourt, 2002.
- *Do Your Ears Hang Low?* by Caroline Church. Chicken House, 2002.
- *Farmer in the Dell* by Pam Adams. Childs-Play International, 2001.
- *How Much Is that Doggie in the Window?* by Iza Trapani. Charlesbridge Publishing, 1997.

- *I'm a Little Teapot* by Iza Trapani. Charlesbridge Publishing, 1996.
- *Itsy Bitsy Spider* by Iza Trapani. Charlesbridge Publishing, 1993.
- *Oh, Where, Oh Where Has My Little Dog Gone?* by Iza Trapani. Charlesbridge Publishing, 1995.
- *Seals on the Bus* by Lenny Hort. Henry Holt & Company, 2000.
- *This Old Man* by Pam Adams. Childs-Play International, 1990.
- *Twinkle, Twinkle, Little Star* by Iza Trapani. Charlesbridge Publishing, 1994.
- *Wheels on the Bus* by Paul O. Zelinksy. Dutton, 1990.

Literature Pictures (LPs) for Joseph Had a Little Overcoat

Photocopy to desired size.

Quilt Me a Story · Lesson 2

Featured Book

Something from Nothing: Adapted from a Jewish Folktale by Phoebe Gilman. Scholastic, 1993.

In this retelling of a traditional Jewish folktale, Joseph's baby blanket is transformed into ever smaller items as he grows until there is nothing left. But then Joseph has an idea. ISBN 0590472801

Lesson Learning Ideas

Literature Appreciation

- Participates in investigating character analysis
- Is familiar with the fictional format of a cumulative story

Techniques of Learning

- Has experience with compare and contrast questioning
- Understands and participates in brainstorming activities
- Uses organizational formats for learning

Writing Experiences

- Has participated in a variety of age-appropriate writing experiences
- Imitates models of good writing
- Indicates an understanding of story structure necessary for narrative writing
- Participates in narrative writing experiences
- Has experience with examples of narrative writing and its uses

Materials

- *Something from Nothing* by Phoebe Gilman book and/or video presentation (see Ordering Information, page 149)
- *Joseph Had a Little Overcoat* by Simms Taback
- Story Frame worksheet (page 63)
- crayons

Before Class

1. Decide on the method of display for the comparison chart and the Story Frame worksheet. Both should be visible for the whole class.

2. Copy enough Story Frame worksheets for each pair or group of students to have one.

Lesson Plan

1. Read aloud *Something from Nothing* or show the 23-minute video. Draw the students' attention to the mice in the pictures and what they are doing with the scraps that are discarded.

2. Compare *Joseph Had a Little Overcoat* with this story. Be sure to mention that in each story the person who received the items was a boy or man.

3. Ask the students to make a comparison chart of everything that was made in each story.

Joseph Had a Little Overcoat	Something from Nothing
overcoat	blanket
jacket	jacket
vest	vest
scarf	tie
necktie	handkerchief
handkerchief	button
button	story
book	

Joseph Had a Little Overcoat	Something from Nothing

4. Ask the students to create a list of things that could be made if the main character was a woman or girl. Place the items in the order they would appear in a similar story. Decide on a name for the main character in the class story. Use the Story Frame to create a class story. Allow the students to work in groups to create the illustrations for their version of the story.

Story Frame

_____ had a little _____.

It got old and worn. So she made a _____

out of it and _____.

_____ had a little _____.

It got old and worn. So she made a _____

out of it and _____.

_____ had a little _____.

It got old and worn. One day there was nothing left but a tiny thread. What could she do with a single thread? Ah, yes, she had just enough to weave a story.

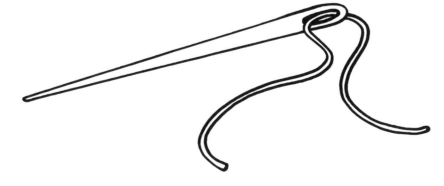

Quilt Me a Story · Lesson 3

Featured Book

The Patchwork Quilt by Valerie Flournoy. Dial, 1985.

Using scraps cut from the family's old clothing, Tanya helps her grandmother and mother make a beautiful quilt that tells the story of a family's life.
ISBN 0803700970

Lesson Learning Ideas

Techniques of Learning

- Has experience in critical thinking questioning

- Has the opportunity to work in cooperative groups

- Is able to integrate cues from written and visual text

- Uses organizational formats for learning

Comprehension

- Has experience in the comprehension strategy of retelling

- Can recall, summarize and paraphrase what is listened to and viewed

Materials

- *The Patchwork Quilt* by Valerie Flournoy

- *The Patchwork Quilt* video (see Ordering Information, page 149)

- *The Patchwork Quilt* Story Pieces (pages 66–67)

- construction paper

- scissors

Before Class

1. Tape the Reading Rainbow program for this lesson. It can be taped and used for educational reasons for one year. Otherwise, follow the ordering directions on page 149 to obtain a permanent copy.

2. Copy and cut apart the story pieces to use with the timeline.

Lesson Plan

1. Show the Reading Rainbow eight-minute segment of *The Patchwork Quilt*. (Reading Rainbow presentations are not word-for-word depictions of the text.) As the children listen, ask them to pay special attention to information that shows that time is passing. Ask the children to share how long Grandma said it would take to make the quilt. *(At least a year.)*

2. Read aloud the first paragraph from the book. When did the story begin? *(Spring)* Create a class timeline that starts with the spring months and extends for one year.

3. Present the Story Pieces one at a time and have the students decide where they would fit on the timeline. (In the story the quilt took until the next June to create. Let the children come to the conclusion that they will have to extend the timeline beyond the one year mark.) Return to the statement that the quilt would take a year at least. Make sure students understand what that means.

4. If students encounter problems with placing the pieces on the timeline, have them return to the book. Doing a picture search will help them put the pieces in order. (The Story Pieces on pages 66–67 are in the order they appeared in the story.)

5. Give each pair of students scissors and scrap construction paper to work with. Instruct each pair to cut 42 small squares from construction paper. Play a game called Count on Quilts. To play, ask the students:

    - to name and count the members of Tanya's family from the story *(6)*

    - to show how many quilt squares Tanya would have if each family member contributed four squares *(24)*

    - what the quilt would look like if Tanya had 42 squares and she wanted to put six squares in each row *(6 x 7)*

    - to show four different ways Tanya could arrange the squares to make a quilt if she has only 12 squares to make a quilt *(2 x 6, 6 x 2, 3 x 4, 4 x 3, 1 x 12, 12 x 1)*

The Patchwork Quilt Story Pieces

Grandma was sitting in her favorite spot—the big soft chair in front of the picture window. In her lap were scraps of materials of all textures and colors. Tanya recognized some of them. The plaid was from Papa's old work shirt, and the red scraps were from the shirt Ted had torn that winter.

"Whatcha gonna do with all that stuff?" Tanya asked.

"Stuff? These ain't stuff. These little pieces gonna make me a quilt, a patchwork quilt."

"We'll have to get you a new pair and use these old ones for rags," Mama said as she hung the last piece of wash on the clothesline one August afternoon.

Jim was miserable. His favorite blue corduroy pants had been held together with patches; now they were beyond repair.

"Bring them here," Grandma said.

Grandma took part of the pant leg and cut a few blue squares.

The arrival of autumn meant school and Halloween. This year Tanya went as an African princess. She danced around in the long, flowing robes Mama made from several yards of colorful material. Grandma cut some squares out of the leftover scraps and added Tanya to the quilt, too!

Only once did Mama put it aside. She wanted to wear something special Christmas night so she bought some gold material and made a beautiful dress. Tanya knew without asking that the gold scraps would be in the quilt too.

New Year's Day was the beginning. After the dishes were washed and put away, Tanya and Mama examined the quilt. "You cut more squares, Tanya, while I stitch some of the patches together," Mama said.

Every day, as soon as she got home from school, Tanya worked on the quilt. But after a few weeks she stopped. Something was wrong—something was missing, Tanya thought. That evening, before she went to bed, Tanya tiptoed into Grandma's room, a pair of scissors in her hand. She quietly lifted the end of Grandma's old quilt and carefully removed a few squares.

February and March came and went as Mama proudly watched her daughter work on the last few rows of patches.

One June day Tanya came home to find Grandma working on the quilt again! She had finished sewing the last few squares together; the stuffing was in place, and she was already pinning on the backing.

In the right-hand corner of the last row of patches was delicately stitched, "For Tanya from you, Mama and Grandma."

Quilt Me a Story • Lesson 4

Featured Book

The Quilt by Ann Jonas. Puffin, 1994.

A child's new patchwork quilt recalls old memories and provides new adventures at bedtime. ISBN 0140553088

Lesson Learning Ideas

Literature Appreciation

- Participates in investigating character analysis

Techniques of Learning

- Is able to integrate cues from written and visual text
- Uses organizational formats for learning

Comprehension

- Has experience in the comprehension strategy of retelling
- Has the opportunity to apply the comprehension strategy of story structure
- Can recall, summarize and paraphrase what is listened to and viewed

Writing Experiences

- Has participated in a variety of age-appropriate writing experiences
- Responds to literature in a variety of written formats
- Indicates an understanding of story structure necessary for narrative writing

Oral Language

- Is developing the ability to respond to what is seen and heard

Materials

- *The Quilt* by Ann Jonas (multiple copies if possible)
- Quilt Stories Graphic Organizer visual (page 70)
- art paper and crayons

Before Class

Decide how to display the Quilt Stories Graphic Organizer visual for the whole class to view.

Lesson Plan

1. Provide enough copies of *The Quilt* so every two or three students can share. Read the book aloud as the students follow along.

2. Direct the students' attention to the graphic organizer. Explain that this is a simple book report like one they may do when they are older. Start at the top left-hand corner and have the students help fill in the answers.

3. When the children reach the main character block, challenge them to defend naming Sally, the stuffed animal, as the main character. Then have them support calling the little girl in the story the main character. As a group, come up with a list of requirements for being the main character. For example, the story would not be the same if this character was missing; the character appears in more of the story than any other character; the problem happens to and is solved by the main character.

4. Tell the students that they can use the six items listed in the top two rows to summarize any kind of story. Discuss how knowing these topics can help them remember what a story is about.

5. Allow students to select the information from one square and create a picture to explain the information. When the pictures are finished allow the children to find a partner and share their picture.

Quilt Stories

Title of Book

Author

Illustrator

Main Character: Who?

Main Character: What do you know?

What problem does the character have?

How is the problem solved?

Quilt in Story: What kind?

Quilt in Story: Made from?

Where is the quilt in the story?

What happens to the quilt in the story?

Quilt Me a Story • Lesson 5

Featured Books

A Far-Fetched Story by Karin Cates. Greenwillow Books, 2002.

With a hard winter on the way, Grandmother uses her family's rags and stories to create a cozy quilt. ISBN 0688159389

The Quilting Bee by Gail Gibbons. HarperCollins, 2004.

An introduction to the process of quilt making, including a history of the craft, sample quilt patterns and directions for creating a children's book authors and illustrators quilt. ISBN 0688163971

Lesson Learning Ideas

Techniques of Learning

- Understands and participates in brainstorming activities
- Attends to personal and/or team tasks outside of the whole group setting
- Can transfer learning experiences across multiple situations
- Takes an active role in recomposing visual and written information

Comprehension

- Is able to make connections with prior knowledge and experience

Oral Language

- Is developing the ability to respond to what is seen and heard

Materials

- *A Far-Fetched Story* by Karin Cates
- Grandmother's Refrain visual (page 73)
- *The Quilting Bee* by Gail Gibbons
- squares of drawing paper
- single hole punch
- yarn
- scissors
- crayons
- Library Word Squares (pages 74–75)

Before Class

1. Make a transparency of the Grandmother's Refrain visual.

2. Create quilt squares out of drawing paper for each student to use to make the library quilt.

Lesson Plan

1. Read aloud the title and author of *A Far-Fetched Story*. Ask the children to share what they think "far-fetched" means. Record student responses. Explain that sometimes if you don't understand what you are reading you can keep reading and the explanation will come from the text.

2. Read aloud Grandmother's Refrain from the visual. Have the students practice reading the refrain aloud, too. Draw attention to the punctuation and how it alerts a reader to the way the words were meant to be read. Show the quotation marks and share their meaning with the children. Tell the students that they will be the Grandmother each time it comes to these words in the story. Read the story with the students speaking the refrain.

3. Share *The Quilting Bee*. Then tell the students that they are going to have a quilting bee to create a library quilt.

4. Give each student a half a square of drawing paper. Ask them to color it as if it is a piece of clothing they are wearing. When the squares have been colored divide the students into pairs. Have each pair of students glue their squares together.

5. Give each pair a smaller Library Word Square to glue in the middle of their square. Then draw attention to the word or phrase at the top of each Library Word Square. Words for squares could include: title, author, illustrator, title page, spine and spine label, award winning, characters, fiction, nonfiction, folktale, picture book, wordless book, fable and poetry (see sample squares on pages 74–75). Go around the room and read aloud the term listed on each square. Stop and discuss what the class knows about the topic.

6. When all of the topics have been discussed, instruct the student pairs to draw something on the white part of their quilt square to illustrate the library term listed on the square.

7. When the squares are complete, punch two holes in each side of each square. Attach the squares with yarn to produce a quilt. This works best if the squares are laminated before they are punched and connected. As the students work on their quilt squares, discuss what they think the phrase "far-fetched" means after hearing the story.

Grandmother's Refrain

"Well, that's a far-fetched story!" said Grandmother. "It's a pity but it can't be helped, and I'm afraid we'll have to burn your _____ for firewood."

"Oh, please, no!" begged the _____. It's my favorite _____."

"I know, dearie, but a long, hard winter is coming."

And, slap-bang, Grandmother threw the rag into the empty wood box where she liked to keep one extra armful of firewood for emergencies.

Photocopy to desired size.

Title	Author
Illustrator	**Title Page**
Spine and Spine Label	**Award Winning**
Characters	**Fiction**

Nonfiction	Folktale
Picture Book	Wordless Book
Proper Care of Books	Fable
Poetry	

Quilt Me a Story · Lesson 6

Featured Book

Grandfather Tang's Story by Ann Tompert. Bantam Doubleday Dell, 1990.
Grandfather tells a story about shape-changing fox fairies who try to best each other until a hunter brings danger to both of them. ISBN 0517572729

Lesson Learning Ideas

Techniques of Learning

- Has established visual literacy skills

- Is able to integrate cues from written and visual text

- Attends to personal and/or team tasks outside of the whole group setting

- Takes an active role in recomposing visual and written information

Oral Language

- Is able to listen to and comprehend a variety of oral presentation formats

Materials

- *Grandfather Tang's Story* by Ann Tompert

- 11 plastic sheet protectors

- 11 Tangram Sets for story presentation (page 79)

- multiple Tangram Sets for students (page 79) *(optional)*

- copies of tangram outlines from story (page 80)

- overhead projector and screen

- art paper

- scissors

Before Class

1. Make 11 copies of the Tangram Set on page 79 from construction paper. Form each of the tangram pictures from the story (page 80) on individual plastic sheet protectors. Simply tape the pieces to the surface of the page protectors. Omit the final tangram picture shown in the book.

2. Practice making a tangram using the directions listed on page 78.

3. *Optional*—Create laminated sets of tangrams (see page 79) in varying colors for student use. Store each set in a plastic sandwich bag.

Lesson Plan

1. Introduce the concept of tangrams. Use the information in the back of *Grandfather Tang's Story* for this lesson. Describe that today's story introduces a new series of lessons. The next few lessons will be about patterned quilts.

2. Show the illustrations in *Grandfather Tang's Story*. Point out how the pictures are shown in traditional illustrations and in tangrams.

3. Read the story while placing the tangram pictures on the overhead as they occur in the story. Discuss why this story is a good introduction to patterned quilts.

4. Give each student a set of pre-cut tangrams, or have the students create their own sets. If you choose to have the students create their own sets of tangrams, lead them through the directions on page 78.

5. See if the students can put the tangram pieces into a square. If they experience problems provide the outline from page 79 and have them copy the square.

6. Give each group a different picture from the story. Give them time to create the tangram either on top of the outline or beside it.

7. Explain how the tangrams will be included in the free reading area.

Tangram Directions

1. Give each student an 8½" x 11" piece of construction paper and a pair of scissors.

   Hold the paper horizontally. Fold the upper left corner down to the bottom edge. Cut off the extra 2½" on the right side of the paper.

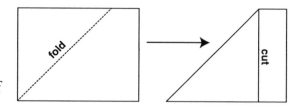

2. Unfold the remaining square and cut along the fold line to make two large triangles.

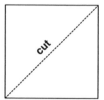

3. Fold one triangle in half. Unfold and cut along the fold line to form two smaller triangles. Set the two shapes aside.

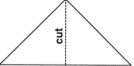

4. Hold the other large triangle with the long edge on the bottom. Fold the top point down to touch the center of the bottom edge. Unfold and cut along the fold line. Set the triangle shape aside.

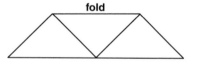

5. Fold the trapezoid in half so the bottom corners meet. Unfold and cut along the fold line.

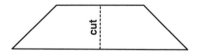

6. Take one half of the trapezoid and fold point A in so it touches the opposite corner, point B. Unfold and cut along the fold line. Set the triangle and square shapes aside.

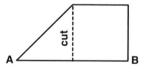

7. Take the other half of the trapezoid and bring the bottom left corner, point C, to the top, point D, to form a triangle. Cut along the fold line to create the remaining triangle and parallelogram. Students should now have all seven shapes.

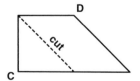

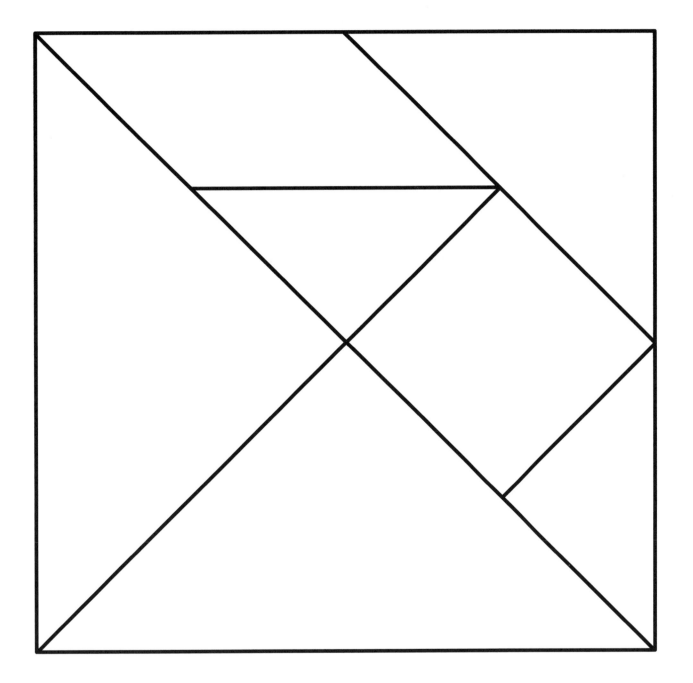

Directions for Making Tangrams

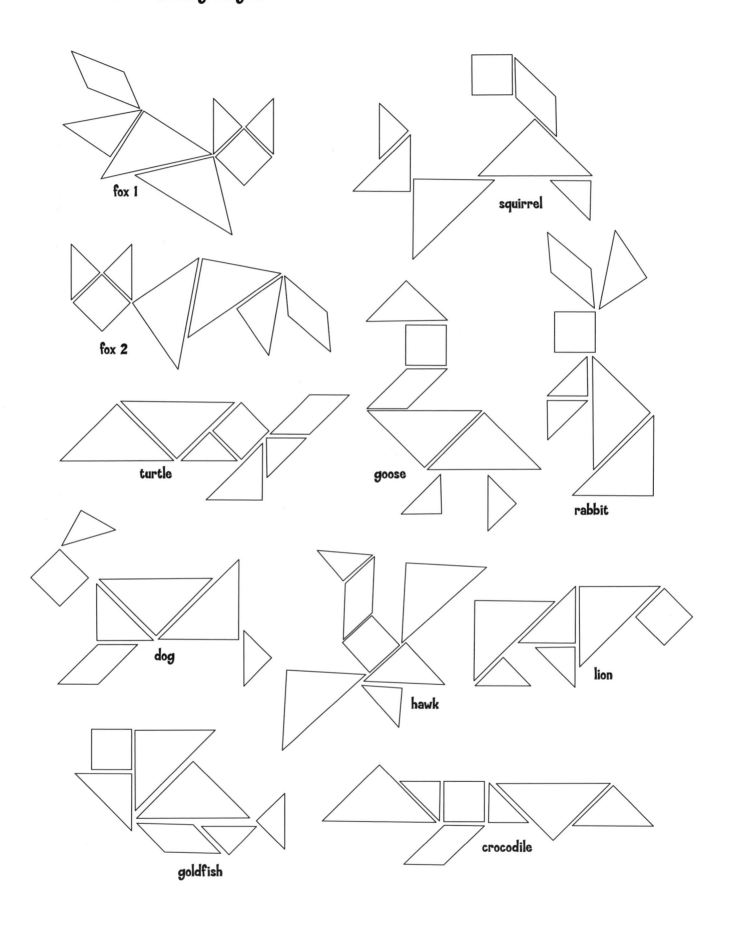

fox 1

squirrel

fox 2

turtle

goose

rabbit

dog

hawk

lion

goldfish

crocodile

Quilt Me a Story · Lesson 7

Featured Book

Sam Johnson and the Blue Ribbon Quilt by Lisa Campbell Ernst. HarperCollins, 1983.

While mending the awning over the pig pen, Sam discovers he enjoys sewing the various patches together but meets with scorn and ridicule when he asks his wife if he could join her quilting club. ISBN 0688015166

Lesson Learning Ideas

Techniques of Learning

- Has established visual literacy skills

- Has the opportunity to work in cooperative groups

- Is able to integrate cues from written and visual text

- Can transfer learning experiences across multiple situations

- Attends to personal and/or team tasks outside of the whole group setting

Comprehension

- Has extended personal vocabulary

- Has enhanced personal sight word vocabulary

- Has the opportunity to participate in experiences that support the acquisition of fluency

- Is able to make connections with prior knowledge and experience

Writing Experiences

- Imitates models of good writing

- Has experience with examples of narrative writing and its uses

Oral Language

- Is developing the ability to respond to what is seen and heard

Materials

- *Sam Johnson and the Blue Ribbon Quilt* by Lisa Campbell Ernst
- quilt of the squares used to tell the story *(optional)*
- Sailboat and Flying Geese patterns (page 83)
- Worn Out Word Quilt visual (page 84)
- *Time for Bed, the Babysitter Said* by Peggy Perry Anderson
- crayons

Before Class

1. The quilt square that frames each illustration tells the story with its name. A quilt can be made using the quilt squares. A list of the designs used is found on the last page of the book. In this way the quilt can be used to tell the story.

2. Copy a sailboat pattern for each girl and a flying geese pattern for each boy.

3. Create a class-sized visual for the Worn Out Word Quilt.

Lesson Plan

1. *Sam Johnson and the Blue Ribbon Quilt* is told with illustrations and quilt patterns. Share how the pictures in this book are like *Grandfather Tang's Story.* Use the book or the quilt squares to tell the story. Show the book to explain where the quilt patterns came from.

2. Give each girl in the class a sailboat quilt square and each boy a flying geese quilt square. Have the children color their quilt squares. Demonstrate how the two patterns were put together to make the Flying Sailboat Quilt.

3. Remind students that worn-out clothes and other scraps of material were used to make a quilt. Tell them that today they are going to make a class quilt of the worn-out word "said." Explain that authors try to vary the words they use to indicate someone said something. Authors do this to keep their writing exciting and to better explain how something is said.

4. Show the Worn Out Word Quilt visual. Walk back through the story and see if students can locate words the author used for "said" in this story. Encourage the children to watch for quotation marks that indicate someone is talking.

   Page 7 exclaimed*

   Page 9 protested*   chuckled nervously*

   Page 10 said calmly*

   Page 15 he began   his voice became louder*   answered a small chorus   he finished

   Page 18 they agreed

Page 27 Sam moaned*   they said to each other   Sam cried*

Page 32 thinking then replied*

5. Suggest that the students might want to consider using other words for "said" as they write. Select one of the starred words from the list and ask for student volunteers to say "hello" using the indicated meaning. For example, have someone say "Hello," calmly. Continue until all of the starred words have been demonstrated.

6. Return to *Time for Bed, the Babysitter Said* from lesson 3 in Focus on Frogs. Have students say "No" using the starred words.

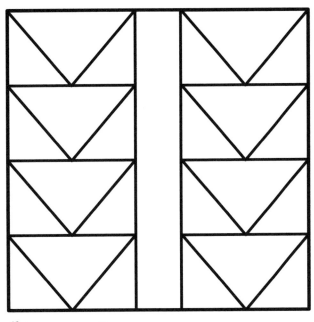

flying geese pattern

sailboat pattern

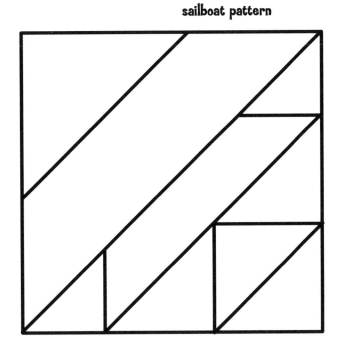

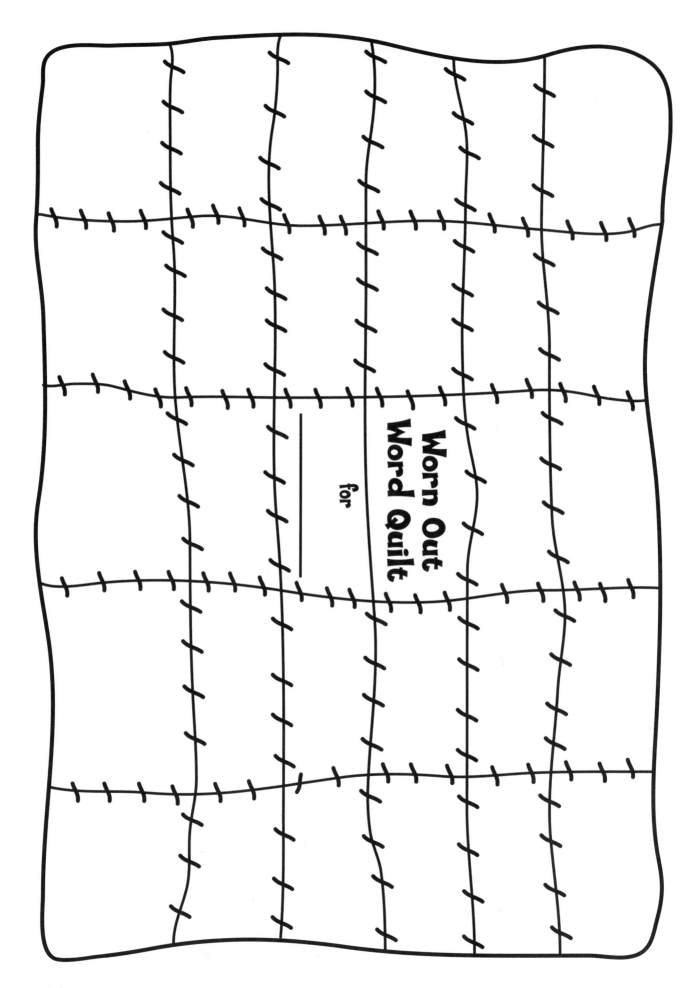

Worn Out
Word Quilt

for

_____

Quilt Me a Story • Lesson 8

Featured Book

The Quiltmaker's Gift by Jeff Brumbeau. Scholastic, 2000.

When a generous quiltmaker agrees to make a quilt for a greedy king under certain conditions, she causes him to undergo a change of heart. ISBN 1570251991

Lesson Learning Ideas

Library Skills

- Uses multiple resources to locate information

Literature Appreciation

- Has used fiction and nonfiction materials
- Has an initial understanding of the difference between fiction and nonfiction

Techniques of Learning

- Has established visual literacy skills
- Has experience in critical thinking questioning
- Understands and participates in brainstorming activities
- Is able to integrate cues from written and visual text

Comprehension

- Has extended personal vocabulary
- Utilizes the comprehension strategy of prediction

Materials

- *The Quiltmaker's Gift* by Jeff Brumbeau
- *Quilts from the Quiltmaker's Gift* by Joanne Larsen Line (Scholastic, 2001)
- *More Quilts from the Quiltmaker's Gift* by Joanne Larsen Line (Scholastic, 2003)
- *The Quiltmaker's Journey* by Jeff Brumbeau
- quilt squares to go with the story *(optional)*

Before Class

As with *Sam Johnson and the Blue Ribbon Quilt* this story can be told through the names of the quilt blocks on each page. If possible, create the quilt block from each page using cloth or paper.

Lesson Plan

1. Show the first page of *The Quiltmaker's Gift* with the quiltmaker working on a quilt. Share the book summary from page 85. Write down the words "generous" and "greedy." Have the children brainstorm the meaning for each of the words. Make sure that the meanings are accompanied by an explanation of why a student thinks his or her meaning fits.

2. Read *The Quiltmaker's Gift* aloud. Return to the words and see if the students would like to add or delete anything. If accurate definitions are not forthcoming use a dictionary or provide your own student-friendly explanations.

3. Direct the students' attention to the paragraph on the inside back of the dust jacket or the last page of the book. Discuss what type of projects might be included.

4. Ask the students what type of book this story is: fiction, nonfiction or biography. Then share *Quilts from the Quiltmaker's Gift* and *More Quilts from the Quiltmaker's Gift*. Ask the students what kind of books these books represent.

5. Share the pictures of the quiltmaker from the fiction story. Lead students in brainstorming about what might have led the quiltmaker to the life she demonstrated in the story.

6. If time allows, read aloud *The Quiltmaker's Journey* and explain what the term prequel means.

7. There are numerous activities to supplement this story. Pick and choose from the following list:

   - Share the picture from the inside cover of the dust jacket and allow students to search for the hidden pictures. Ask why the paper cover on a book is called a dust jacket.

   - Visit the Web site *www.QuiltmakersGift.com* and select one or more of the activities for participation. This a must-see Web site!

   - Use the names of the quilt blocks listed on the endpapers. Give the students a quilt block name and ask them to guess where in the story the quilt block appears. Check the answers using the book.

Quilt Me a Story · Lesson 9

Featured Book

Eight Hands Round: A Patchwork Alphabet by Ann Whitford Paul. HarperCollins, 1991.

Introduces the letters of the alphabet with names of early American patchwork quilt patterns and explains the origins of the designs by describing the activity or occupation from which they are derived. ISBN 0060246898

Lesson Learning Ideas

Techniques of Learning

- Has established visual literacy skills
- Has experience in critical thinking questioning
- Is able to integrate cues from written and visual text
- Uses organizational formats for learning
- Attends to personal and/or team tasks outside the whole group setting
- Takes an active role in recomposing visual and written information

Comprehension

- Is able to make connections with prior knowledge and experience
- Can recall, summarize and paraphrase what is listened to and viewed

Oral Language

- Is developing the ability to respond to what is seen and heard

Materials

- *Eight Hands Round* by Ann Whitford Paul
- Quilt Patterns (page 89)
- Quilt Glyph Directions (page 90)
- pictures of several quilt squares from *Eight Hands Round*

Before Class

1. Make multiple copies of the Windmill and Bowtie Quilt Patterns.

2. Decide how to share the Quilt Glyph Directions (transparency, individual paper copies or chart) and create.

3. Make several Quilt Glyphs for examples.

4. Use paper or cloth to create several of the quilt squares from *Eight Hands Round*. (Churn Dash; Hole in the Barn Door; Grandmother's Fan; Rising Sun; Flying Geese; Log Cabin; Necktie, Bow Tie, True Lovers' Knot; Windmill, Whirlwind; and Variable Star.)

Lesson Plan

1. Select several quilt square patterns from *Eight Hands Round* that have appeared in other stories in this unit. Tell the story behind each pattern. See if the students can remember another name of the quilt square and/or what story it appeared in.

2. Read the description of the Yankee Puzzle. Ask the students if they remember a book that had puzzles in it. *(Grandfather Tang's Story)*

3. Present several pre-made quilt block glyphs as examples of the quilt glyphs the students will create. Refer to page 39 for more specific instructions on presenting glyphs.

4. Allow time for all of the students to complete their quilt block glyph. Post all of the glyphs so everyone can see them. Then start with one criterion and build on it, letting the students use the glyph information to analyze the data. Data analysis might include:
   - How many students are an only child? (one criterion)
   - How many students have an even number of people in their family? (one criterion)
   - How many students have brothers and an odd number of people in their family? (two criteria)
   - How many students came into their family second, fourth or sixth and have an even number of people in their family? (two criteria)

Quilt Patterns

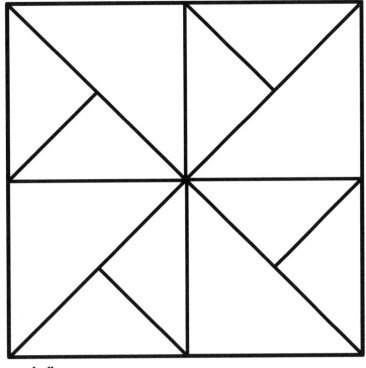

windmill pattern

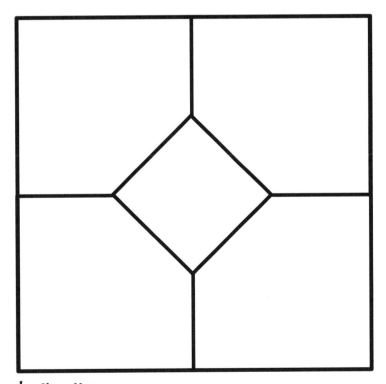

bowtie pattern

Quilt Glyph Directions

Name: _____

Day: _____ Month: _____

Date: _____ Year: _____

1. **Number of people in your family**

Quilt Square	When to Use
Windmill	Even number of people
Bowtie	Odd number of people

2. **Kinds of siblings (brothers and sisters)**

Decoration	When to Use
Hearts	Only child
Stars	Brothers
Dots	Sisters

3. **Order in which you came into the family**

Color	When to Use
Red and Yellow	Came into the family as the first, third or fifth child
Blue and Green	Came into the family as the second, fourth or sixth child

Quilt Me a Story • Lesson 10

Featured Book

Let's Make Rabbits by Leo Lionni. Knopf, 1992.

Two rabbits made with a pencil and scissors become real after eating a real carrot. ISBN 0679826408

Lesson Learning Ideas

Library Skills

- Can identify the title, author and illustrator

- Can identify the spine and spine label of a book

- Knows the spine label tells where a book is placed on the shelf

- Can locate and identify the basic parts of a book

Literature Appreciation

- Has used fiction and nonfiction materials

- Has an initial understanding of the difference between fiction and nonfiction

Techniques of Learning

- Has the opportunity to work in cooperative groups

- Can transfer learning experiences across multiple situations

- Attends to personal and/or team tasks outside the whole group setting

Comprehension

- Is able to make connections with prior knowledge and experience

Materials

- *Let's Make Rabbits* by Leo Lionni

- example of an appliqué quilt

- Patterns for Appliqué Rabbit (pages 94–95)

- Book Spine Cards (pages 96–99)

- scissors, glue and wallpaper scraps

- *My Four Lions* by Bernice Gold (Annick Press, 1999) *(optional)*

Before Class

1. Most stores that sell wallpaper will give the outdated books to schools to use for art projects. Check with local stores well in advance of needing the materials.

2. Make enough copies of pages 94 and 95 so that each student will be able to make a rabbit.

3. Make the Rabbit Match Game by copying the cover and title page from all of the books in the unit. Use all four of the books from Lesson 8.

4. Add the appropriate call numbers from your library to the Book Spine Cards. Copy and cut out each card.

Lesson Plan

1. Explain that so far the stories have been about patchwork and pattern quilts. Today's lesson is a story to prepare the students for books about appliqué quilts. Bring back the quilt or quilt square you showed at the beginning of the unit that represented appliqué quilts. Allow time for students to speculate how making appliqué quilts differs from making the other quilts they have seen.

2. Read aloud *Let's Make Rabbits*. When the story is over ask the students to decide which rabbit was the better example of an appliqué rabbit. Encourage students to provide reasons for their guesses.

3. Provide each student with the rabbit pattern pieces. Also give each group of students pencils, scissors, glue, white paper and several different scraps of wallpaper. Demonstrate how to trace around the pattern onto the wallpaper and cut it out. Explain that this is the way quilts are made. Walk through the entire process before students start to work. Provide enough time for the children to complete the task.

4. Demonstrate how to play the Rabbit Match Game by showing one matching book cover and title page. Tell the students they are going to play a game where they will try to make a match like the example. Explain that if they get a book cover they will be looking for the matching title page and if they get a title page they will be looking for the matching book cover.

5. Hand out a book cover or title page to each student. Tell them to look at their sheet but not to show it to anyone. When all the students have one, have them stand up and—without talking—find their match.

6. Display the Book Spine Cards. Have each set of student pairs select the card that matches their book.

7. Check the students' answers. Ask if the children can see any pattern in the spine labels for fiction books. Ask if they see any pattern in the spine labels for nonfiction books. Teach the students the chant "Numbers mean nonfiction."

8. Discuss the parts of a book cover, spine and title page. As each part is mentioned have each student pair point to the item on their cards.

9. If time permits, have the students create a list of things in their lives that are real and things that are make-believe. If necessary, supplement the discussion by using *My Four Lions* by Bernice Gold. This book shows a realistic story and a fantasy version within the same story.

Patterns for Appliqué Rabbit

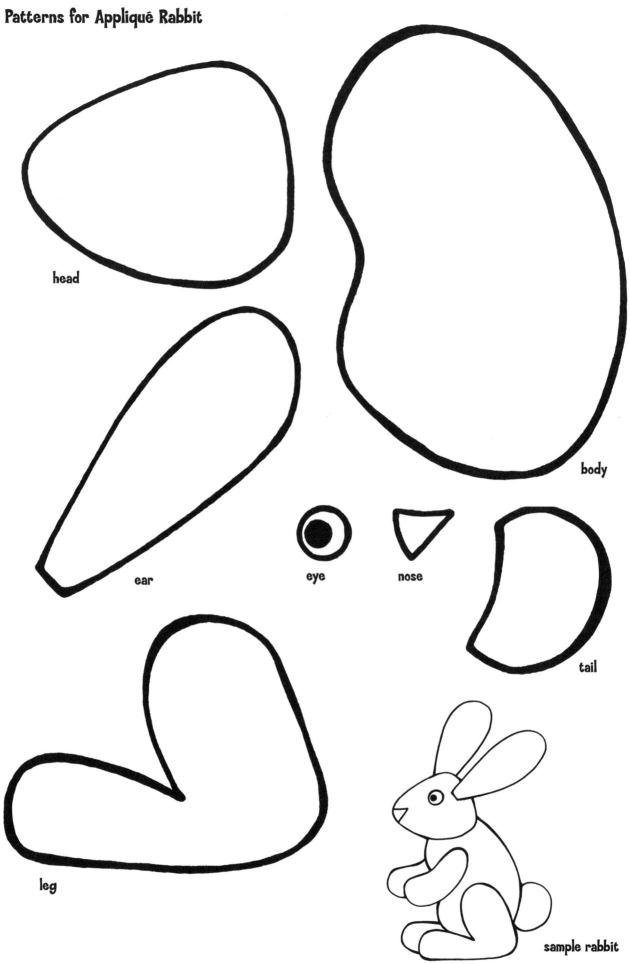

head

body

ear

eye

nose

tail

leg

sample rabbit

Today in the library we read
Let's Make Rabbits by Leo Lionni!
See the appliqué rabbit that I made.

Name: _____

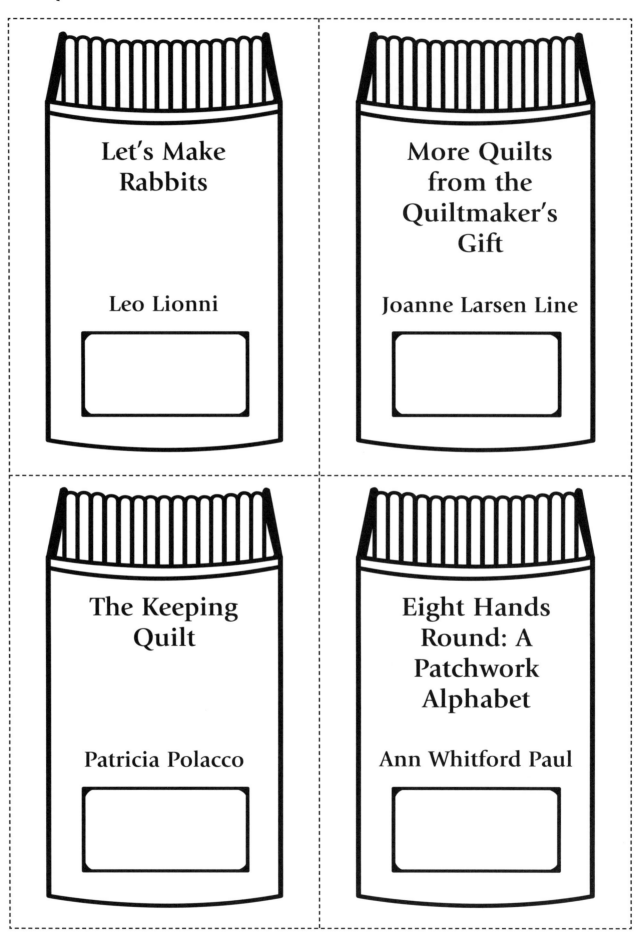

Let's Make
Rabbits

Leo Lionni

More Quilts
from the
Quiltmaker's
Gift

Joanne Larsen Line

The Keeping
Quilt

Patricia Polacco

Eight Hands
Round: A
Patchwork
Alphabet

Ann Whitford Paul

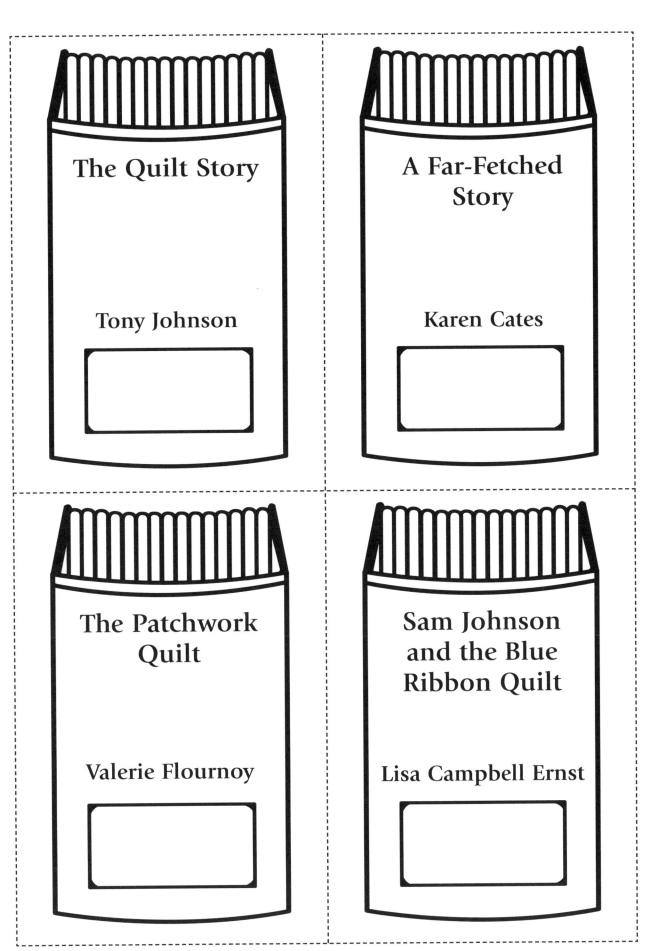

The Quilt Story

Tony Johnson

A Far-Fetched Story

Karen Cates

The Patchwork Quilt

Valerie Flournoy

Sam Johnson and the Blue Ribbon Quilt

Lisa Campbell Ernst

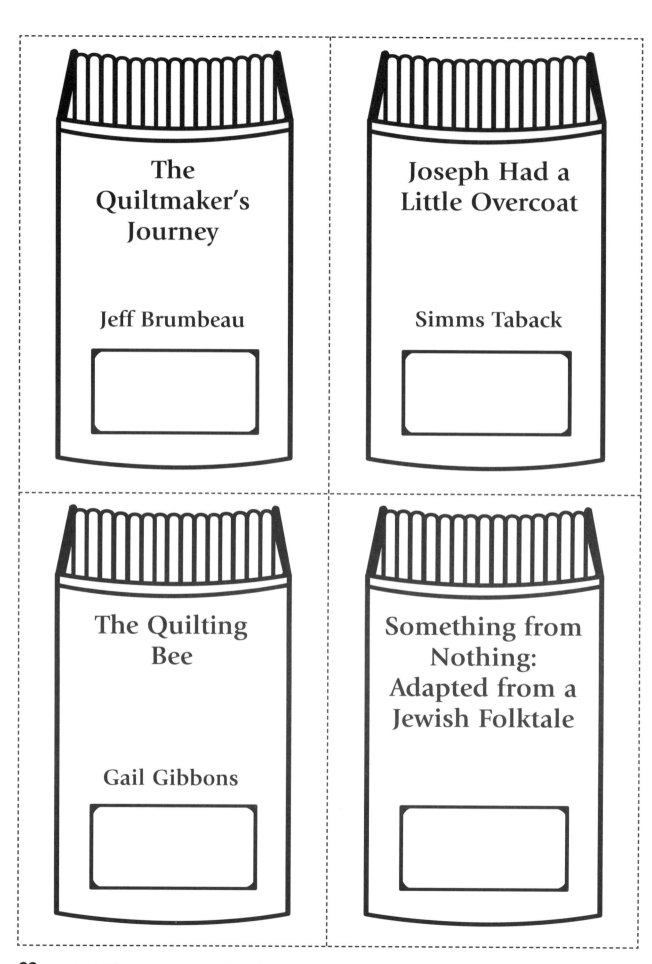

The
Quiltmaker's
Journey

Jeff Brumbeau

Joseph Had a
Little Overcoat

Simms Taback

The Quilting
Bee

Gail Gibbons

Something from
Nothing:
Adapted from a
Jewish Folktale

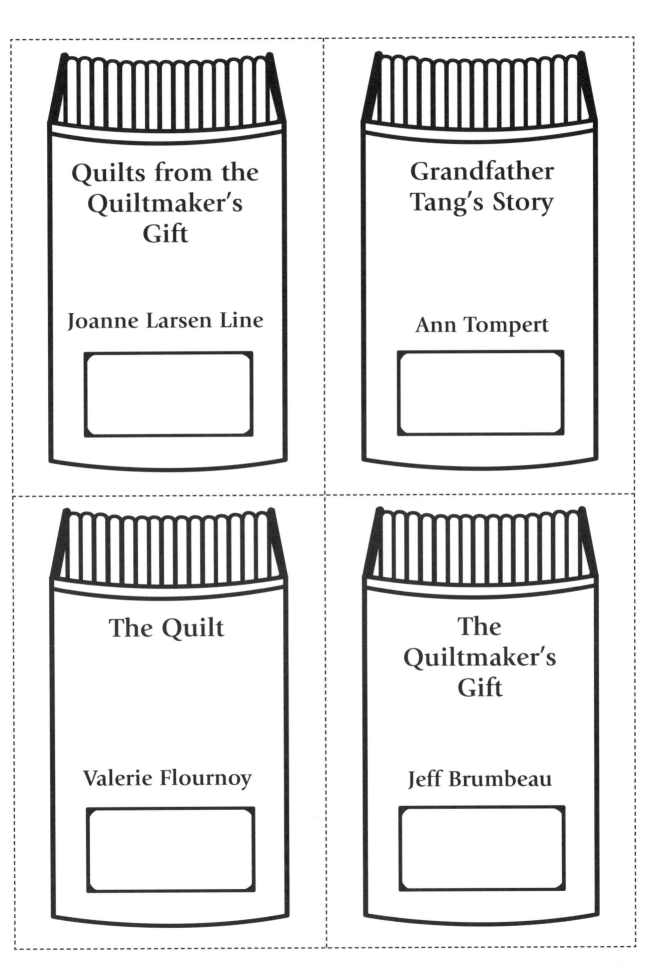

Quilts from the Quiltmaker's Gift

Joanne Larsen Line

Grandfather Tang's Story

Ann Tompert

The Quilt

Valerie Flournoy

The Quiltmaker's Gift

Jeff Brumbeau

Quilt Me a Story • Lesson 11

Featured Book

The Quilt Story by Tony Johnston. Putnam, 1985.

A pioneer mother lovingly stitches a beautiful quilt, which warms and comforts her daughter Abigail; many years later another mother mends and patches it for her little girl. ISBN 0399210091

Lesson Learning Ideas

Techniques of Learning

- Has established visual literacy skills

- Has experience in critical thinking questioning

- Has experience with compare and contrast questioning

- Is able to integrate cues from written and visual text

Comprehension

- Has experience in the comprehension strategy of retelling

- Is able to make connections with prior knowledge and experience

- Can recall, summarize and paraphrase what is listened to and viewed

Oral Language

- Is developing the ability to respond to what is seen and heard

Materials

- *The Quilt Story* by Tony Johnston big book (see Ordering Information, page 150)

Before Class

Make copies of four pictures from the book: the two different pictures of quilts from the story (one is in the front of the book and one is in the back), the picture of the little girl in front of the pioneer home and the picture of the modern-day family standing in the doorway of their new home.

Lesson Plan

1. Read aloud from the big book version of *The Quilt Story.*

2. Share that this is really two stories in one, which is easy to miss if you don't focus on the pictures. Draw attention to the first picture that shows the mother and daughter together. Ask students to look closely at the clothes and try to decide when this story took place. If students do not grasp that this is a pioneer story show other pictures from the beginning of the story. Another example might be the picture of the wagon train.

3. Share the pictures of the little girls and their new homes. Ask the children to compare the pictures and decide the time period that the pictures depict. Once the children realize that the story shows two different little girls with the same quilt, turn the pages and summarize the text until the students find the turning point in the story.

4. Ask the students to look at the two pictures of the quilt. Have the children discuss which they think is the quilt at the beginning of the story and which is the quilt at the end of the story. If students struggle with the concept of old and new, approach the subject using the terms old and new. Have the children describe which quilt is the old version and which is the new version. Then ask when in the story the quilt was new and when it was old. To verify the conclusion, show which quilt is shown in the front of the book and which is in the back.

5. Return to the illustrations and have the students look for the cat that appears in many of the pictures. Ask if it is the same cat in all of the pictures. Why not?

6. Select one or two pictures and let the children tell the story segment from the cat's point of view. This may take a good deal of modeling to accomplish.

Quilt Me a Story • Lesson 12

Featured Book

The Keeping Quilt by Patricia Polacco. Simon & Schuster, 1988.

A homemade quilt ties together the lives of four generations of an immigrant family, remaining a symbol of their enduring love and faith.
ISBN 0671649639

Lesson Learning Ideas

Library Skills

- Uses multiple resources to locate information

- Is familiar with basic reference books and their purpose

Literature Appreciation

- Has an understanding of the concept of artist and illustrator

- Has an understanding of how authors write books

Techniques of Learning

- Has experience in critical thinking questioning

- Understands and participates in brainstorming activities

Comprehension

- Is developing the ability to generate appropriate questions

Writing Experiences

- Has participated in a variety of age-appropriate writing experiences

Materials

- *The Keeping Quilt* by Patricia Polacco book and video (for video, see Ordering Information, page 150)

- *Firetalking* by Patricia Polacco (Richard C. Owen Publishers, 1994)

- other books by Patricia Polacco

- author books with information on Patricia Polacco

- Question Stems visual (page 32)
- *Thank You Mr. Falker* by Patricia Polacco *(optional)*

Before Class

1. Log on to Patricia Polacco's Web site at *www.patriciapolacco.com* and work through the materials available for items to accompany this lesson. Check for pictures to color and puzzles to go with the story the students will share.

2. Gather as many of Patricia Polacco's books as are available in your collection. Check the author books in your collection for information about Patricia Polacco.

3. Use the Question Stems from lesson 5 of Focus on Frogs.

Lesson Plan

1. Show the illustrations in *The Keeping Quilt.* Discuss the use of color in the illustrations with the students.

2. Share the book by showing the 13-minute video version. The video includes an introduction by Patricia Polacco and insight into the creation of the story.

3. Circulate other books by Patricia Polacco. Use the Question Stems visual to help students create questions they might like to have answered about Patricia Polacco. Post the questions for students to see. Then share the Web sites below, *Firetalking* and available author books to try to locate the answers to some of the student questions.

   - *www.ipl.org/div/kidspage/askauthor/polaccobio.html*
     Includes questions children have asked Patricia Polacco.

   - *www.teachervision.fen.com/lesson-plans/lesson-4039.html*
     Includes questions from children and letter-writing ideas concerning Patricia Polacco.

   - *www.emints.org/ethemes/resources/S00000512.shtml*
     Includes numerous Web links to Polacco information.

   - *www.carolhurst.com/titles/keepingquilt.html*
     Includes specific activities for the featured book.

   - *curry.edschool.virginia.edu/go/edis771/webquest2000/student/slindadukes/home.html*

Bug Out Over Books

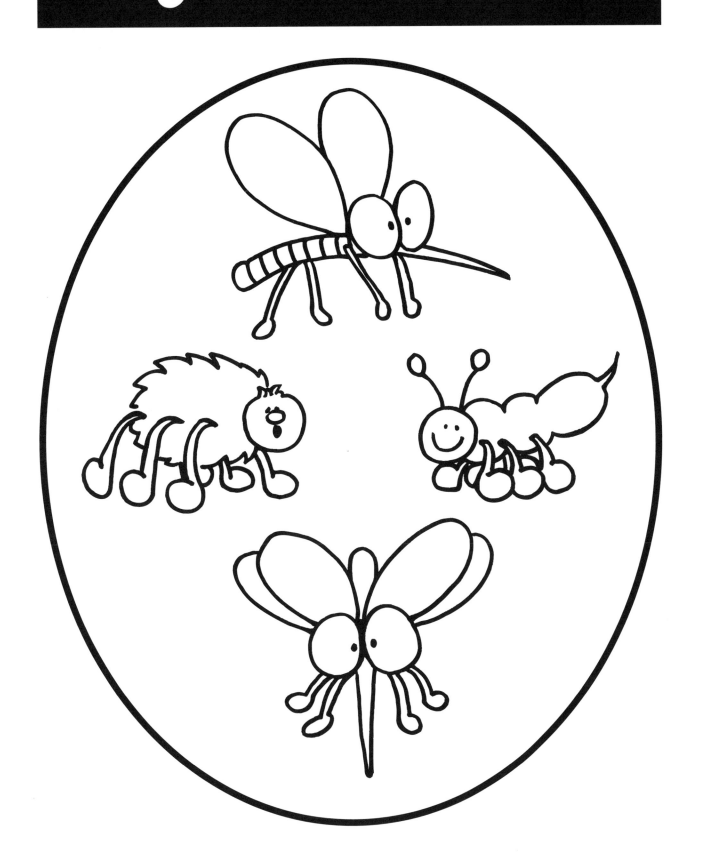

Bug Out Over Books · Lesson 1

Featured Book

Bugs! by David J. Greenberg. Megan Tingley Books, 1997.

Celebrates the disgusting and horrible things you can do with a bunch of bugs. ISBN 0316325740

Lesson Learning Ideas

Literature Appreciation

- Has had experience with various literary genres—poetry

- Has used fiction and nonfiction materials

Techniques of Learning

- Has experience in critical thinking questioning

- Has the opportunity to work in cooperative groups

- Can transfer learning experiences across multiple situations

- Attends to personal and/or team tasks outside the whole group setting

- Takes an active role in recomposing visual and written information

Comprehension

- Has extended personal vocabulary

Oral Language

- Is developing the ability to respond to what is seen and heard

Materials

- *Bugs!* by David T. Greenberg

- *Animal Life for Children—All About Bugs* video (see Ordering Information, page 150)

- index cards

- markers

- art supplies

- category cards (page 108)

Before Class

1. Preview the video so you know where to stop the tape for this lesson's segment.

2. Copy the category title cards shown below.

Lesson Plan

1. Have the class create a list of all the creatures they believe are bugs. List each suggestion on a separate index card.

2. Read aloud *Bugs!* Return to the student list to see if the children want to add any other names. After the students have exhausted their ideas, introduce the category cards.

3. Instruct the students to listen carefully to the video for clues about the difference between bugs and bugs that are insects. Play the first part of the video *Animal Life for Children—All About Bugs.* Show from the beginning of the video to the Animal Inquiries segment (approximately seven minutes).

4. Return to the category cards and see if the children understand that insects are a subgroup of bugs. You could also explain that all insects are bugs but not all bugs are insects. Ask the students to create a list of the characteristics of insects ("3-2-3" is a good way to remember—all insects have three sets of legs, two antennae and three body parts). Save this list to use throughout the unit.

5. Divide the children into small groups. Challenge each group to create a song/chant, poster or drama that will remind them what 3-2-3 means. Give students the time and materials to produce their reminder. Randomly select groups to present.

Bugs

Bugs that Are Insects

Bug Out Over Books • Lesson 2

Featured Book

Insects 1 by John Bonnett Wexo. Wildlife Education, Ltd., 2000.

Discusses the beauty, variety, importance and miniature world of insects. Includes index. Part of the Zoobooks series. ISBN 1888153555

Lesson Learning Ideas

Library Skills

- Uses multiple resources to locate information

- Is developing a basic concept of the research process

Literature Appreciation

- Has used fiction and nonfiction materials

Techniques of Learning

- Has the opportunity to work in cooperative groups

- Is able to integrate cues from written and visual text

- Can transfer learning experiences across multiple situations

- Attends to personal and/or team tasks outside of the whole group setting

- Takes an active role in recomposing visual and written text

Writing Experiences

- Has participated in a variety of age-appropriate writing experiences

- Responds to literature in a variety of written formats

- Participates in expository writing experiences

Oral Language

- Is developing the ability to respond to what is seen and heard

Materials

- *Insects 1* by John Bonnett Wexo (multiple copies to use throughout the unit, see Ordering Information, page 150)

- *Animal Life for Children—All About Bugs* video

- Backyard Bugs (see Ordering Information, page 150)

- list of insect characteristics (from lesson 1)

- Incredible Insect Insights Learning Log (page 111)

Before Class

1. Preview the video so you know where to start and stop for this lesson's segment.

2. Divide the plastic bugs into sets of six—one of each bug (spider, fly, caterpillar, dragonfly, grasshopper and beetle) and place them in ziplock bags.

3. Make a journal cover for each student. Insert blank pages on which students may write and draw. If there are multiple first grade classes, make all of the journal covers for each class from a different color of paper.

Lesson Plan

1. Read aloud page two from *Insects 1*. Discuss the characteristics of insects. Have the students revisit their list of insect characteristics and see if they want to make any changes.

2. If possible, show the two-minute video segment from *Animal Life for Children—All About Bugs* that reviews the characteristics of insects. This part starts immediately after the Animal Inquiries segment and ends when the discussion turns to spiders.

3. Give each pair of students a set of plastic bugs. Let each group try to decide which of these bugs they think are insects. When students have had time to make their decision, lead a discussion to determine the answers. (Insects: dragonfly, beetle, fly and grasshopper.) As a creature is proven to be an insect, place the index card with that insect's name in the correct category. Those that do not fit can be placed in the bugs category. (As students find information throughout the unit they can try to prove if a creature on their master list is an insect or not.)

4. Hand out an Incredible Insect Insights Learning Log to each student. Explain that throughout the unit they will have the opportunity to return to their book to record their thoughts and pictures about what they are studying. Give the children time to decorate the cover and write their name and classroom teacher's name on the back.

5. If time permits allow the students to record their thoughts and pictures about the characteristics of insects using information from the group discussion.

Name: _____

Teacher: _____

Incredible
Insect Insights

Learning Log

Bug Out Over Books • Lesson 3

Featured Book

The Napping House by Audrey Wood. Harcourt, 1984.

In this cumulative tale, a wakeful flea atop a number of sleeping creatures causes a commotion, with just one bite. ISBN 0152567089

Lesson Learning Ideas

Library Skills

- Uses multiple resources to locate information

- Is developing a basic concept of the research process

- Can locate and identify the basic parts of a book

Literature Appreciation

- Has used fiction and nonfiction materials

- Has an initial understanding of the difference between fiction and nonfiction

Techniques of Learning

- Has experience in critical thinking questioning

- Has the opportunity to work in cooperative groups

- Attends to personal and/or team tasks outside of the whole group setting

- Takes an active role in recomposing visual and written information

Comprehension

- Is beginning to comprehend basic text structures

Writing Experiences

- Has participated in a variety of age-appropriate writing experiences

- Can create labels, notes and/or captions

- Responds to literature in a variety of written formats

- Participates in descriptive writing experiences

Materials

- *Insects 1* by John Bonnett Wexo
- *The Napping House* by Audrey Wood (see Ordering Information, page 150)
- *Flea* by Karen Hartley, Chris Macro, Philip Taylor and Alan Fraser (Heinemann Library, 2000)
- art paper and crayons

Before Class

Nothing needed.

Lesson Plan

1. Share with the students that in the following lessons they will be introduced to books about insects. Some of the books will be fiction and some will be nonfiction. Review the meaning of these words.

2. Introduce the first creature for study with a series of clues. Share one clue at a time and have a few students try to guess the insect. Continue with clues and guesses until some-one guesses the correct answer. Provide the original list of insects or display several of the books from the Bug Book series to assist the students in guessing the insect for study.

   Clue One: If you've got an itch I might be the key.
   Clue Two: I'm very hard to see.
   Clue Three: Dogs don't like me.
   Clue Four: My name rhymes with key, see and me.
   Answer: Flea

3. Have students turn to a partner and discuss what they know about fleas. After ample time for discussion, create a list of things students know about fleas.

4. Read aloud from *The Napping House*. Ask the students why it might be said that the flea is the main character in the story. Direct the discussion by asking how the story would be different if the flea was not in the story.

5. Turn to any two-page spread in *The Napping House*. Ask the students to look closely and name as many of the items in the picture that they see. Write down the items that the children list. Assign each student one of the words from the picture. (Write the responsible child's name beside the word on the list.)

6. Instruct the children to draw a picture of the item and to write the name of the item on their paper. As the students finish their pictures encourage them to write down an explanation of what the item is. Circulate around the room to assist students with their writing.

7. When the children are finished, have them help put the words in alphabetical order. Then explain that they have created a glossary for *The Napping House*. Briefly explain

what a glossary is and where they are found. Encourage the children to look for books in the nonfiction section that have a glossary.

8. Show the picture of a flea from page 4 in *Flea*. Tell the students to notice how ordinary the shape of a flea is. Then read aloud pages 6 and 7 in *Insects 1*. Direct students' attention to each photograph and read the corresponding caption.

9. Have students turn back to their partners and see if they can come up with one clue that relates to one of the pictures on page 6 or 7 in *Insects 1*. Review the clues used at the beginning of the class if necessary. Let several student pairs share their clues and see if the other students can guess which insect they are talking about.

 Bug Out Over Books • Lesson 4

Featured Book

The Flea's Sneeze by Lynn Downey. Henry Holt & Company, 2000.

A flea with a cold startles all the animals in the barn when it sneezes unexpectedly. ISBN 0805061037

Lesson Learning Ideas

Literature Appreciation

- Has used fiction and nonfiction materials

Techniques of Learning

- Has experience with compare and contrast questioning
- Attends to personal and/or team tasks outside of the whole group setting
- Takes an active role in recomposing visual and written information

Writing Experiences

- Has participated in a variety of age-appropriate writing experiences
- Responds to literature in a variety of written formats
- Uses prewriting strategies such as drawings, brainstorming and/or graphic organizers
- Participates in expository writing experiences

Oral Language

- Is developing the ability to respond to what is seen and heard

Materials

- *Insects 1* by John Bonnett Wexo
- *The Flea's Sneeze* by Lynn Downey
- *The Flea's Sneeze* Literature Pictures (pages 116–121)
- Venn Diagram visual (page 122)
- Incredible Insect Insights Learning Logs (page 111)
- *The Napping House* by Audrey Wood

Before Class

1. Make one set of *The Flea's Sneeze* Literature Pictures to use when presenting the story to the students. Follow the directions on page 10.

2. Make several sets of the Literature Pictures for the free reading center.

3. Create a class-size Venn Diagram visual to use in the book comparison.

Lesson Plan

1. Read *The Flea's Sneeze* using the Literature Pictures on a metal board or Velcro apron.

2. Share the Venn Diagram visual to promote a comparison of *The Napping House* and *The Flea's Sneeze*. Compare the stories based on the characters, setting, etc. Next ask students what other comparisons they might make using a Venn diagram to help them organize their thinking. Take all answers and have the children share how a Venn diagram could be used with each suggestion.

3. Explain that fleas do not have wings. Ask students how they think fleas move around.

4. Share pages 14 and 15 of *Insects 1*. Read each caption as the children study the photographs.

5. Hand out the students' learning logs and encourage them to write and/or draw about anything from the current lesson. Have the students brainstorm things they might include before starting to work.

Literature Pictures (LPs) for The Flea's Sneeze

Photocopy to desired size.

Literature Pictures (LPs) for The Flea's Sneeze

Venn Diagram

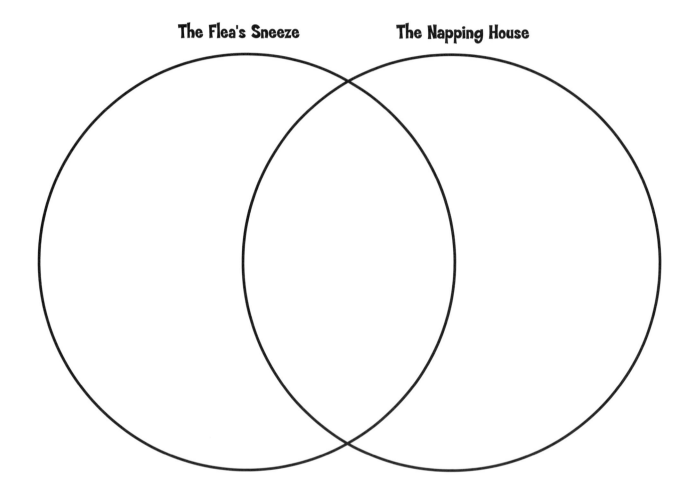

The Flea's Sneeze

The Napping House

Bug Out Over Books · Lesson 5

Featured Book

Flea by Karen Hartley, Chris Macro, Philip Taylor and Alan Fraser. Heinemann Library, 2000.

An introduction to fleas, including what they look like, how they are born, what they eat, how they grow and where they live. ISBN 1575725479

Lesson Learning Ideas

Library Skills

- Uses multiple resources to locate information
- Is developing a basic concept of the research process
- Can locate and identify the basic parts of a book

Literature Appreciation

- Has used fiction and nonfiction materials
- Understands and applies nonfiction reading techniques

Techniques of Learning

- Has experience in critical thinking questioning
- Uses organizational formats for learning
- Attends to personal and/or team tasks outside of the whole group setting
- Takes an active role in recomposing visual and written information

Comprehension

- Has experience in the comprehension strategy of retelling
- Can recall, summarize and paraphrase what is listened to and viewed
- Is beginning to comprehend basic text structures

Writing Experiences

- Has participated in a variety of age-appropriate writing experiences
- Can create labels, notes and/or captions
- Responds to literature in a variety of written formats
- Uses prewriting strategies such as drawings, brainstorming and/or graphic organizers

Materials

- *Flea* by Karen Hartley, Chris Macro, Philip Taylor and Alan Fraser

- list of insect characteristics from Lesson 4

- Insect Characteristics Data Grid (page 125)

Before Class

1. Make enough copies of the Insect Characteristics worksheet so each pair of students has one.

2. Make a class-size copy of the Insect Characteristics worksheet to use with each class.

Lesson Plan

1. Reintroduce *Flea* from lesson 3. Read aloud the first chapter. Ask students where on the category chart the flea should be located. Once you have established how they know that the flea is an insect, gather other information about this insect.

2. Check to make sure students understand that *Flea* is a nonfiction book. Clarify that when reading a factual book the reader does not always read the book from beginning to end as with a fiction story. Focus the children's attention on the Table of Contents. Tell them that for this lesson they will be looking for information about the characteristics of an insect as they relate to a flea.

3. Read the chapter headings one at a time and ask the children to decide which chapters they think would be the best places to find information on what fleas look like. The chapters selected might include: What do fleas look like? How big are fleas? How do fleas move? Include any suggested chapters even if they end up not producing any facts for the grid. Students will learn that not all leads produce the results wanted.

4. Provide each pair of students with a copy of the Insect Characteristics worksheet. Explain that when looking for information, people need to know what they are looking for before they start.

5. Read aloud one chapter at a time from the selected chapters. At the end of each chapter ask if there are any facts to place on the Insect Characteristics Data Grid. Write in the facts on the class grid as student partners fill in their own grids.

6. If more information is needed to fill in the grid, assist students in locating other sources of information. The following back issues of *Ranger Rick* magazine have information on fleas: November 1993, July 1996, July 1997, July 2001, January 2002 and September 2002.

Insect Characteristics

Data Grid for _____

Head and Antennae	Legs
Abdomen/Shape/Color	**Thorax and Wings**

Other

Bug Out Over Books • Lesson 6

Featured Book

Flea by Karen Hartley, Chris Macro, Philip Taylor and Alan Fraser. Heinemann Library, 2000.

An introduction to fleas, including what they look like, how they are born, what they eat, how they grow and where they live. ISBN 1575725479

Lesson Learning Ideas

Library Skills

- Uses multiple resources to locate information

- Is developing a basic concept of the research process

Techniques of Learning

- Uses organizational formats for learning

- Is able to integrate cues from written and visual text

Comprehension

- Has experience in the comprehension strategy of retelling

- Can recall, summarize and paraphrase what is listened to and viewed

Writing Experiences

- Has participated in a variety of age-appropriate writing experiences

- Is able to generate brief descriptions that use sensory details

- Is able to transfer ideas into sentences with appropriate support

- Participates in expository writing experiences

Materials

- *Flea* by Karen Hartley, Chris Macro, Philip Taylor and Alan Fraser

- magazines, trade and reference books on fleas from your collection

- Insect Characteristics Data Grid (page 125)

- Fantastic Flea Facts worksheet (page 128)

Before Class

1. Gather materials from your library collection on fleas.

2. Make a class-size copy of the Fantastic Flea Facts worksheet to use with each class.

3. Make a copy of the Fantastic Flea Facts worksheet for each pair of students.

4. Post the Insect Characteristics Data Grid from the last lesson.

Lesson Plan

1. Review the information from the data collected during the last session. Use additional sources to fill out the information in the grid if needed. Explain to the children that together they will use the information to write a report about fleas.

2. Hand out a Fantastic Flea Facts worksheet to each pair of students. Share that the class is going to create a report using the letters of the word "flea" as a guide. The report will include one or two sentences about each of the items listed in the frame.

3. Start with "flat bodies" and ask the children to check the Data Grid to see if they have any information about a flea's flat body. If there is information, have the students compose one or two sentences about the facts. If there is not information on the grid, skip it for now and move through the frame filling in all that is available from the Data Grid. Enter the information on the Fantastic Flea Facts visual as the student partners copy the same information onto their frames.

4. After the frame has been covered one time, return to the items where more information is needed. Instruct students to search their sources again, this time looking specifically for the missing information. Finally, have the whole class complete the report.

Fantastic Flea Facts

F – flat bodies _____

_____

_____

L – legs _____

_____

_____

E – eyes _____

_____

_____

A – antennae _____

_____

_____

S – sharp spines _____

_____

_____

Bug Out Over Books • Lesson 7

Featured Book

The Bee Tree by Patricia Polacco. Philomel, 1993.

To teach his granddaughter the value of books, a grandfather leads a growing crowd in search of the tree where the bees keep all their honey.
ISBN 039921965X

Lesson Learning Ideas

Literature Appreciation

- Has used fiction and nonfiction materials

- Has an initial understanding of the difference between fiction and nonfiction

- Is familiar with the fictional format of a cumulative story

Techniques of Learning

- Has experience in critical thinking questioning

Writing Experiences

- Responds to literature in a variety of written formats

- Is able to transfer ideas into sentences with appropriate support

- Participates in expository writing experiences

Materials

- *The Bee Tree* by Patricia Polacco

- *Thank You, Mr. Falker* by Patricia Polacco (Philomel, 1998)

- *Insects 1* by John Bonnett Wexo

- *The Bee Tree* Literature Pictures (pages 131–134)

- *Animal Life for Children—All About Bugs* video

- *Bee* by Karen Hartley and Chris Macro (Heinemann, 1998)

- Incredible Insect Insights Learning Logs

- *Thank You, Mr. Falker* video (see Ordering Information, page 150)

Before Class

1. Make the Literature Pictures into a metal board presentation. Follow the directions on page 10.

2. Preview the video to make sure where to start and stop the tape for this lesson's segment. Start the video with the picture of the green caterpillar. The narrator says: "So like all other animals bugs need to eat."

3. Make multiple copies of the Literature Pictures to add to the free reading center.

Lesson Plan

1. Read/tell *The Bee Tree* by Patricia Polacco. Use the Literature Pictures to enhance the presentation. Add these materials to the free reading materials.

2. Share that the author of today's story also wrote *The Keeping Quilt,* which was studied in the quilt story unit.

3. Introduce the students to another Polacco story, *Thank You, Mr. Falker.* (This book is also available as a 26-minute video from Spoken Arts.) Share at least the end of *Thank You, Mr. Falker* to provide the children with the connection that the two books share. Discuss why the books are considered fiction, although they are based on Polacco's life.

4. Discuss that today's story represents a cumulative story. Allow the students to speculate on the meaning of "cumulative." Provide a student friendly explanation that might include creating a parallel to the word "accumulation" as it relates to snow predictions. Most children understand that when there is a significant accumulation of snow, it is more likely that school will be canceled.

5. Redirect the students' attention to factual information. Show the *Animal Life for Children—All About Bugs* video segment that discusses the way insects eat. Stop the video when the discussion turns to insects in the larger world.

6. Read aloud from pages 4 and 5 of *Insects 1*. This section discusses insect bodies and the way they eat. As a final piece for this lesson, introduce *Bee*. Read aloud pages 26 and 27 from the chapter "How are Bees Special?" Explain that this book will be used in the next lesson.

7. Give out the Incredible Insect Insights Learning Logs and allow the students to write and/or draw about anything from the unit on insects. Let the students brainstorm things they might include before starting to work.

Literature Pictures (LPs) for The Bee Tree

Photocopy to desired size.

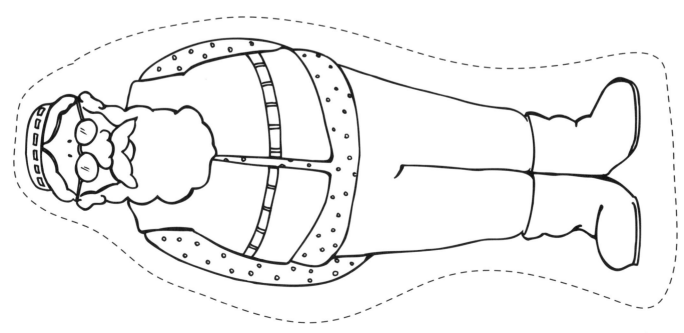

# Bug Out Over Books • Lesson 8

Featured Book

Bee by Karen Hartley and Chris Macro. Heinemann Library, 1998.

A simple introduction to the physical characteristics, diet, life cycle, predators, habitat and lifespan of bees. ISBN 1575726610

Lesson Learning Ideas

Library Skills

- Uses multiple resources to locate information
- Is developing a basic concept of the research process

Literature Appreciation

- Has used fiction and nonfiction materials
- Understands and applies nonfiction reading techniques

Techniques of Learning

- Has the opportunity to work in cooperative groups
- Can transfer learning experiences across multiple situations
- Attends to personal and/or team tasks outside of the whole group setting

Comprehension

- Is able to set a purpose for reading
- Can recall, summarize and paraphrase what is listened to and viewed
- Is beginning to comprehend basic text structures

Materials

- *Bee* by Karen Hartley and Chris Macro (multiple copies)
- table of contents from *Bee*
- Insect Characteristics Data Grid (page 125)
- books from your library collection that include information about bees
- Incredible Insect Insights Learning Logs (page 111)

Before Class

1. Make enough copies of the table of contents from *Bee* for each pair of students. The students will write on this copy.

2. Make enough copies of the Insect Characteristics worksheet for each pair of students.

3. Make a class-size copy of the Insect Characteristics worksheet.

Lesson Plan

1. Discuss the steps that were followed to find information on fleas:

   A. Checked the table of contents to find chapters that would most likely provide the information needed.

   B. Read the chapters selected as having the most potential.

   C. Used a data grid to record facts/information.

   D. Used information from the data grid to create a report on fleas.

2. Explain to the children that this time the topic for investigation will be bees, but they will follow the same steps. Make sure the students understand that these steps can be used anytime they are looking for information.

3. Tell the students that they will do most of the work with a partner. Give each pair of students a copy of the table of contents from *Bee*. Read aloud the chapter headings. (All of the books in the Bug Book series have the same format; that is why they were selected to introduce students to research techniques.) Once again the search is for information about the characteristics of bees. As the headings are read aloud have the students put a plus or minus symbol next to each heading. Use the plus sign to indicate a chapter that might be useful. Use the minus sign to indicate a chapter that might not include much useful information. Remind students that there may be differences of opinion.

4. Tally the results to find the chapters the students think are most likely to provide the information they are looking for. Read aloud one chapter at a time. At the end of each chapter ask if there are any facts they want to add to the grid. Provide each pair with a data grid to fill in for themselves. (If there are enough books so that each pair of students has one, they will be able to complete more of the writing on their own because it will be in front of them.)

5. If more information is needed, assist students in locating other sources of information. The following issues of *Ranger Rick* magazine have information on bees: February, August, September, November and December 1997; November 1999; January, May and August 2002; and April 2003.

6. Ask the students to state one fact they learned about insects during this unit. Make a list on the board or a chart. Give out the student learning logs and have them write down one fact, then draw a picture and write a sentence or two about the fact.

Bug Out Over Books · Lesson 9

Lesson Learning Ideas

Library Skills

- Uses multiple resources to locate information
- Is developing a basic concept of the research process

Techniques of Learning

- Has the opportunity to work in cooperative groups
- Can transfer learning experiences across multiple situations
- Attends to personal and/or team tasks outside of the whole group setting

Comprehension

- Has extended personal vocabulary
- Is beginning to comprehend basic text structures

Writing Experiences

- Has participated in a variety of age-appropriate writing experiences
- Can create labels, notes and/or captions
- Is able to generate brief descriptions that use sensory details
- Responds to literature in a variety of written formats
- Uses prewriting strategies such as drawings, brainstorming and/or graphic organizers
- Imitates models of good writing
- Is able to transfer ideas into sentences with appropriate support
- Participates in expository writing experiences

Materials

- *Insects 1* by John Bonnett Wexo
- *Bee* by Karen Hartley and Chris Macro

- picture of honeybee from the National Wildlife Federation Web site *(www.nwf.org/kidzone)*
- magazines, trade and reference books on bees from your collection
- Insect Characteristics Data Grid (page 125)
- Bee Report form (page 139)

Before Class

1. Log on to *www.nwf.org/kidzone.* Click on "Your Big Backyard: Ages 3–7," select "Coloring Pages" from the left side, then "Honeybee" from "Insects, Spiders and More." Print the picture of the honeybee and make a copy for each pair of students.

2. Check the children's search engine called Kids Click! at *sunsite.berkeley.edu/ KidsClick!/* for current, age-appropriate Web sites on bees for students to use.

3. Gather materials from your library collection on bees.

4. Make enough copies of the Bee Report form for each pair of students and make a class-size copy.

5. Post the Insect Characteristics worksheet from the last lesson.

Lesson Plan

1. Review the Insect Characteristics worksheet from the last session. Tell the children that together they will use the information to make a report about bees.

2. Show pages 4 and 5 from *Insects 1.* Ask students how the information is presented. Lead them to see that information is provided in photographs, drawings, text and diagrams. If any of these terms are unfamiliar to the students discuss their meanings and give examples before moving on to the next step.

3. Provide each pair of students with a copy of the bee picture from the Web site. Ask the students to label all of the parts listed in the grid. Walk through this as a class by choosing one part from the grid, then deciding how and where to label it on the picture.

4. Allow students to use other reference materials to add information to their drawing. When this is complete, provide time for students to share. Make sure the children include where they found the information in order to prove its validity.

5. Hand out the Bee Report to each pair of students. Explain that the class is going to create a counting report for their bee information. Return to the Data Grid to find things that will fit into the frame. If there are missing pieces return to the sources to look for specific information. Allow the students to complete as much as they can on their own. A suggested completed report has been included on page 140.

Bee Report

With a bee

It is easy to see

A half dozen or so

Facts you need to know.

Bees have one _____.

Bees have two _____.

Bees have three _____.

Bees have four _____.

Bees have five _____.

Bees have six _____.

So there you go.

Do you know

Any more

About bees?

Bee Report

With a bee

It is easy to see

A half dozen or so

Facts you need to know.

Bees have one <u>tongue</u>.

Bees have two <u>antennae</u>.

Bees have three <u>body parts</u>.

Bees have four <u>wings (two pair)</u>.

Bees have five <u>eyes</u>.

Bees have six <u>legs</u>.

So there you go.

Do you know

Any more

About bees?

Bug Out Over Books · Lesson 10

Featured Book

Why Mosquitoes Buzz in People's Ears: A West African Tale retold by Verna Aardema. Dial, 1975.

Mosquito tells Iguana such a tall tale that Iguana puts sticks in his ears so he won't have to hear. This causes a chain of events that upsets all of the animals and leads to an explanation of why mosquitoes buzz in people's ears. ISBN 0803760892

Lesson Learning Ideas

Literature Appreciation

- Is familiar with the fictional format of a cumulative story

Techniques of Learning

- Is able to integrate cues from written and visual text
- Attends to personal and/or team tasks outside of the whole group setting
- Takes an active role in recomposing visual and written information

Comprehension

- Is able to make connections with prior knowledge and experience
- Can recall, summarize and paraphrase what is listened to and viewed
- Is beginning to comprehend basic text structures

Writing Experiences

- Responds to literature in a variety of written formats
- Uses prewriting strategies such as drawings, brainstorming and/or graphic organizers
- Is able to transfer ideas into sentences with appropriate support
- Participates in expository writing experiences

Oral Language

- Is developing the ability to respond to what is seen and heard

Materials

- *Insects 1* by John Bonnett Wexo

- *Why Mosquitoes Buzz in People's Ears: A West African Tale* retold by Verna Aardema

- *Why Mosquitoes Buzz in People's Ears: A West African Tale* video (see Ordering Information, page 150)

- other fiction books from this unit

- Incredible Insect Insights Learning Logs

Before Class

Nothing needed.

Lesson Plan

1. Explain that today's book is a way of explaining why mosquitoes make a buzzing sound. It is said that only the male makes the buzzing sound and they don't bite. It is the female who is silent but who is widely known for her bite.

2. Show the 10-minute video *Why Mosquitoes Buzz in People's Ears.*

3. See if the students can list the names of the three other fiction books that were presented in this unit. Remind them of the insects that were in these stories. Tell the students that all of these stories are called cumulative stories. Discuss how the characters and the action in each story accumulates.

4. Switch the attention to *Insects 1*. Share pages 16 and 17. Before reading, ask the children what they think this information will be about. Read aloud the text and captions that go with the pictures.

5. Ask the students to state one fact they learned about insects during this unit. This should be a different fact from the one they used in their last journal entry. Make a list on the board or a chart.

6. Hand out the Learning Logs and instruct students to write down one fact. Have them draw a picture and write a sentence or two about their fact. Ask each student to relate that fact to his or her life in some way. Suggest that they consider what the fact makes them think about or how it makes them feel. Model this process by taking a fact or two and indicating how you would respond. Have the students practice with a partner. Depending on the experience of the students there may be a need for quite a bit of practice before expecting the students to do this alone.

Bug Out Over Books • Lesson 11

Featured Books

The Beetle Alphabet Book by Jerry Pallotta. Charlesbridge Publishing, 2004.
Uses letters of the alphabet to introduce various kinds of beetles. ISBN 1570915520

The Icky Bug Alphabet Book by Jerry Pallotta. Charlesbridge Publishing, 1986.
Introduces the characteristics and activities of insects and other crawly creatures from A to Z, beginning with the ant and concluding with the zebra butterfly. ISBN 0881064505

The Icky Bug Counting Book by Jerry Pallotta. Charlesbridge Publishing, 1992.
A counting book with facts and illustrations of insects. ISBN 0881064963

Insects: A Three-Part Story by Robin Bernard. National Geographic Society, 2001.
Introduces common insect characteristics. ISBN 0792294254

Lesson Learning Ideas

Techniques of Learning

- Is able to integrate cues from written and visual text
- Can transfer learning experiences across multiple situations

Comprehension

- Has extended personal vocabulary
- Has experience in the comprehension strategy of retelling
- Utilizes the comprehension strategy of prediction
- Is able to set a purpose for reading
- Is able to make connections with prior knowledge and experience

Writing Experiences

- Can create labels, notes and/or captions
- Is able to generate brief descriptions that use sensory details
- Responds to literature in a variety of written formats
- Uses prewriting strategies such as drawings, brainstorming and/or graphic organizers

- Is able to transfer ideas into sentences with appropriate support
- Participates in descriptive writing experiences

Oral Language

- Is developing the ability to respond to what is seen and heard

Materials

- *Insects: A Three-Part Story* by Robin Bernard (see Ordering Information, page 150)
- *The Beetle Alphabet Book* by Jerry Pallotta (paperback recommended)
- *The Icky Bug Alphabet Book* by Jerry Pallotta (paperback recommended)
- *The Icky Bug Counting Book* by Jerry Pallotta (paperback recommended)
- easy release painters' tape
- Insect Characteristics Data Grid (page 125)
- writing paper
- art supplies

Before Class

1. Use painters' tape to cover the following words in *Insects:* page 1–"isn't" (3 times); page 2–"If you counted three, it probably is an insect!"; page 3–"six" (5 times) and "all insects"; page 6–"wings" and "fly"; page 7–"feelers"; page 11–"hide."

2. If enough copies of the Pallotta books are available, cut them apart, then laminate the pages. This way each page can be used independent of the book.

3. Display the Insect Characteristics worksheet.

Lesson Plan

1. Introduce the big book of *Insects.* Have the students help fill in the missing words. Read and discuss the book.

2. Share the bug books by Jerry Pallotta. Use the pictures from these books and allow the students to locate the illustrations that are insects. Remind the children that the book they just read said that insects were the only animals with six legs.

3. Give each student or each pair of students a picture of one of the insects from the Jerry Pallotta books. Have the children choose one part of the insect from the Insect Characteristics worksheet (Legs; Thorax/Wings; Head/Mouth/Antennae; or Abdomen/Color/Shape).

4. Instruct the students to write a short description of the featured body part and draw an illustration of their insect highlighting the featured body part. Share that in the final lesson the class will create a designer insect.

Bug Out Over Books · Lesson 12

Lesson Learning Ideas

Library Skills

- Uses multiple resources to locate information

- Is developing a basic concept of the research process

Literature Appreciation

- Has used fiction and nonfiction materials

Techniques of Learning

- Has experience in critical thinking questioning

- Has the opportunity to work in cooperative groups

- Understands and participates in brainstorming activities

- Is able to integrate cues from written and visual text

- Uses organizational formats for learning

- Can transfer learning experiences across multiple situations

- Takes an active role in recomposing visual and written information

Comprehension

- Is able to set a purpose for reading

- Is able to make connections with prior knowledge and experience

- Can recall, summarize and paraphrase what is listened to and viewed

Materials

- Create an Insect worksheet (page 147)

- art supplies

- all of the books from the unit

- Pallotta books from lesson 11

Before Class

Make several class-size copies of the Create an Insect worksheet.

Lesson Plan

1. Remind the students that this is the last session on insects and they are going to create their own class insect.

2. Share the class-size copy of the Create an Insect form. Explain that they will choose the different components for their insect.

3. Select an insect picture used in one of the lessons in this unit. Allow the students to complete the grid based on that insect. This will allow for practice with the process. If necessary, complete more than one grid using different insects.

4. Lead the class in making the decisions for their class insect. Then break the students into small groups and tell them to construct a picture of the class insect. This can be a flat picture or a 3-D model. Ask the students to label the parts included on the Create an Insect sheet with their representation. Share the results.

Note: This activity can be done in small groups instead of as a class.

Create an Insect

The insect's name will be _____.

Describe the insect's legs: _____
_____
_____
_____

Describe the insect's head and antennae: _____
_____
_____
_____

Describe the insect's thorax and wings: _____
_____
_____
_____

Describe the insect's abdomen by shape and color: _____
_____
_____
_____

Great Rip Roar Read Report

Pages torn

Pages missing

Written or colored in

Other

Name: _____

🌸 Ordering Information 🌸

Focus on Frogs

Lesson 1

How to Make a Paper Frog: Available from National Geographic School Publishing in paperback six-packs. Order code WE41890.

> National Geographic School Publishing
> P.O. Box 10597
> Des Moines, IA 50340-0597
> 800-368-2728
> *www.ngschoolpub.org*

Elephant Puppet: Available from Folkmanis. Folkmanis puppets can be purchased from several locations, such as M.S. Creations *www.m-s-creations.com.*

Lesson 4

Same-Different Fairy Tales Book: Available for purchase from Kagan Cooperative Learning. The item can be purchased for $12 or in combination with Same–Different Holidays for $20.

> Kagan Cooperative Learning
> P.O. Box 72008
> San Clemente, CA 92673-2008
> 800-933-2667
> *www.kaganonline.com*

Lesson 8

The Caterpillar and the Polliwog Video: Available from Weston Woods.

> Weston Woods
> 143 Main Street
> Norwalk, CT 06851
> 800-243-5020
> Fax 203-845-0498
> *www.scholastic.com/westonwoods*

Lesson 9

Mysterious Tadpole and Trumpet Video Visits Steven Kellogg Videos: Both videos are available from Weston Woods.

> Weston Woods
> 143 Main Street
> Norwalk, CT 06851
> 800-243-5020

> Fax 203-845-0498
> *www.scholastic.com/westonwoods*

Lesson 10

Frog Big Book: Available from Heinemann Classroom. A Shared Reading Pack (six paperback student versions) is also available.

> Heinemann Classroom
> 6277 Sea Harbor Drive, 5th Floor
> Orlando, FL 32887
> 888-363-4266
> *www.heinemannclassroom.com*

Life Cycle of a Frog Plastic Teaching Models: Available from M.S. Creations *(www.m-s-creations. com)* under the title Frog Metamorphic Vinyl Stages with the item number of GBR2. One set of four hands-on manipulatives is available for $5.

Quilt Me a Story

Lesson 1

Joseph Had a Little Overcoat Video: Available from Weston Woods.

> Weston Woods
> 143 Main Street
> Norwalk, CT 06851
> 800-243-5020
> Fax 203-845-0498
> *www.scholastic.com/westonwoods*

Lesson 2

Something From Nothing Video: Available from SVE.

> Clearvue & SVE
> 6465 North Avondale Avenue
> Chicago, IL 60631
> 800-253-2788
> *www.clearvue.com*

Lesson 3

The Patchwork Quilt Video: Available from GPN.

> GPN
> P.O. Box 80669
> Lincoln, NE 68501-0669
> 800-228-4630
> *gpn.unl.edu*

Lesson 11

The Quilt Story Big Book: Available from Scholastic Books.

> Scholastic Books
> 2931 E. McCarty Street
> Jefferson City, MO 65101
> 800-724-6527
> *www.scholastic.com*

Lesson 12

The Keeping Quilt Video: Available from Spoken Arts for $49.95.

> Spoken Arts Videos
> 195 South White Rock Road
> Holmes, NY 12531
> 800-326-4090
> Fax 845-878-9009
> *www.spokenartsmedia.com*

Bug Out Over Books

Lesson 1

Animal Life for Children—All About Bugs Video: Available from Library Video Company.

> Library Video Company
> P.O. Box 580
> Wynnewood, PA 19096
> 800-843-3620
> Fax 610-645-4040
> *www.LibraryVideo.com*

Lesson 2

Zoobooks: Available in magazine/softback versions from Wildlife Education, Ltd.

> Wildlife Education, Ltd.
> 12233 Thatcher Ct.
> Poway, CA 92064-6880
> 858-513-7600
> www.zoobooks.com

Backyard Bugs: A set of 72 plastic bugs in six different shapes. Available from Learning Resources.

> Learning Resources
> 380 N. Fairway Dr.
> Vernon Hills, IL 60061
> 800-333-8281
> *www.learningresources.com*

Lesson 3

The Napping House Big Book: Available from Follett Library Resources.

> Follett Library Resources
> 1340 Ridgeview Drive
> McHenry, IL 60050
> 888-511-5114
> Fax 800-852-5458
> *www.titlewave.com*

Lesson 7

Thank You, Mr. Falker Video: Available from Spoken Arts for $49.95.

> Spoken Arts Video
> 195 South White Rock Road
> Holmes, NY 12531
> 800-326-4090
> Fax 845-878-9009
> *www.spokenartsmedia.com*

Lesson 10

Why Mosquitoes Buzz in People's Ears: A West African Tale Video: Available from Weston Woods for $49.95.

> Weston Woods
> 143 Main Street
> Norwalk, CT 06851-0597
> 800-243-5020
> *www.scholastic.com/westonwoods*

Lesson 11

Insects: A Three-Part Story by Robin Bernard: Available from National Geographic School Publishing in three formats: Big Book and Teacher's Guide; Big Book Kit with big book, six standard-size books and Teacher's Guide; or Little Book Classroom pack that contains 10 standard-size books.

> National Geographic School Publishing
> P.O. Box 10597
> Des Moines, IA 50340
> 800-368-2728
> *www.ngschoolpub.org*